Easton's Book
701 So
Moun

SO-AIJ-920

French Letters and
English Overcoats

Also by Richard De'ath and published by Robson Books:

Laws and Disorders: A Law-Breaking Guide to Real but Bizarre Laws from over the Centuries

French Letters and English Overcoats

Sexual Fallacies and Fads from Ancient
Greece to the Millennium

By Richard De'ath

Robson Books

Published in 2000 by Robson Books, 10 Blenheim Court, Brewery
Road, London N7 9NT

Copyright © 2000 Richard De'ath

The right of Richard De'ath to be identified as author of this work
has been asserted by him in accordance with the Copyright,
Designs and Patents Act 1988.

British Library Cataloguing in Publication Data:
A catalogue record for this title is available from the British
Library.

ISBN 1 86105 323 1

All rights reserved. No part of this publication may be reproduced,
stored in a retrieval system, or transmitted in any form or by any
means, electronic, mechanical, photocopying, recording or otherwise, without the prior permission in writing of the publishers.

'There is no norm in sex. Norm is the name of the guy who lives in Brooklyn.'

ALEX COMFORT,
Medical World News, *November 1974.*

'Never go to bed with anyone crazier than yourself.'
KRIS KRISTOFFERSON,
The Observer, *July 1998.*

CONTENTS

$\mathcal{A}$CKNOWLEDGEMENTS

I would like to acknowledge my debt to a number of doctors, physicians and other members of the medical profession who would probably rather *not* be mentioned by name for their help in the compiling of this book. Together they pointed me towards the well-documented follies and foolishness of their predecessors that enliven these pages.

I am also grateful to the various newspapers, magazines and periodicals which have allowed me to quote from them and which are given due credit in the text. During the course of my research I consulted a number of medical histories and I must record my indebtedness to the following: *The Anxiety Makers* by Alex Comfort (1967), *The Folklore of Sex* by Albert Ellis (1951), *Sex, Sin and Sanctity* by John Langdon-Davies (1954), *Sex in History* by G. Rattray Taylor (1953), *Sex, Society and History* by Vern L. Bullogh (1976) and *The Irresistible Impulse* by Norman Gelb (1979). I also drew material from the various writings of William Acton, Florence E. Barrett, Edward Carpenter, Louise Creighton, August Forel, Walter Heape, Mrs S. Herbert, Kenneth Ingram, Arabella Kenealy, Anthony M. Ludovici, Charles Thompson, William I. Thomas, Ralph De Pomerai, H. Fehlinger, Paul Ferris, E. S. Turner, A. S. E. Ackerman, Edward Gregersen, James Leslie McCary, Richard Gordon, James McDonald, Alan Bestic, Alan Wykes, Rodney Dale, Daniel W. Hering, Philip Ward and Edgar Gregersen.

The illustrations in this book are all from my own private collection – but that is a secret between you and me.

Richard De'ath
January 2000

Hornbooks of The Appetites

An Introduction

Priapische Romane

*

III. BAND.

Rom, 1797
bei Seraph Cazzovula.

In the year 1927, Charles Lindbergh became the first man to fly solo across the Atlantic; Al Jolson starred in the first 'talkie', *The Jazz Singer*; and Mae West was jailed for ten months for using 'lewd material' in her play, *Sex*. On a smaller scale, one of Joanna Southcott's mysterious boxes was opened to reveal an antique pistol, various trinkets, a night cap and a book, *The Surprises of Love*; the Institute of Trichologists – hairdressers, in case you don't know – announced that long hair for women and beards and moustaches for men were out of fashion; and William H. Smyth published a little book with the very curious title *Did Man and Woman Descend from Different Animals?*

Smyth, an Englishman whose main claim to fame was as the engineer who invented technocracy, was, in fact, the latest in a very long line of philosophers, physicians, doctors, scientists and not a few laymen who believed they had something new to say about the oldest subject of all: sex. As far back as the time of the ancient Greeks and Romans, mankind had been debating how the sexes came into being: one popular suggestion being that the early 'root races' had actually been hermaphroditic, males and females united in each individual. William H. Smyth had a very different view and said so in his now long-forgotten book.

The fallacies and fads about sex can be traced back virtually to the Garden of Eden and the story that Adam was expelled because he'd performed the sexual act – or at least acquired sexual knowledge – and in so doing had opened the floodgates of passion. His temptation with the apple became the symbol for temptation, and Eve – the temptress – became specifically a sexual temptress. But even these facts were soon embroidered. In no time it was being believed – and is still widely remembered – that menstruation represented the curse imposed on women in punishment for Eve's part in her partner's seduction.

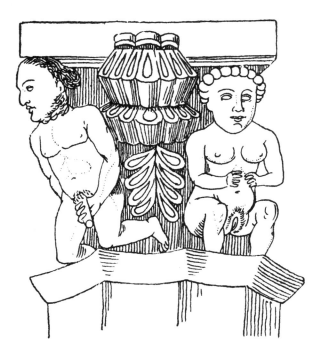

Since the days of the libidinous Greeks and Romans, who somehow found time between their exertions to record the details of their intimate dalliances, sexual fallacies and fads have become a part – not an entirely respectable part, it must be said – of literature. These 'Hornbooks of the Appetite', as one perceptive historian has called them, catalogue mankind's (and womankind's) obsessive interest in sex. Some contained sensible advice, others were mistaken or misinformed, while the rest – whose content form the basis of this book – were just plain wrong: eccentrically, amusingly, even insanely so.

It was that thankfully short-lived Roman emperor, Heliogabalus (AD 204–222), whose gluttony, debauchery and making important staff appointments based solely on the size of an individual's sex organs, got him murdered – yet who also understood the continuing need for information about sex. So one day after solemnly erecting a huge stone phallus and demanding that his citizens worship it, he offered a prize to anyone who could invent a new vice. To the best of my knowledge it is still unclaimed. But it was this quest for knowledge that has inspired subsequent generations of sexologists in their labours about love. During this time, of course, there have been others outraged by the very mention of *that* word – men like the Attorney-General, Sir Thomas Inskip, who remarked while prosecuting a long-forgotten work in 1935: 'This book deals with what everybody will recognise as an unsavoury subject – gratification of sexual appetite.'

Humour, conscious or unconscious, has been an ingredient to be found in so many sex manuals and abounds in these pages with stories of the absurd, the ridiculous and, occasionally, the mad. The sections focus on, respectively (though not always respectably): the famous sex books and their often lacklustre pearls of wisdom; male and female sexual equipment; the art of love-making (in and out of bed) and making it better; the terrible 'sin' of masturbation; the ingenious and varied means of avoiding

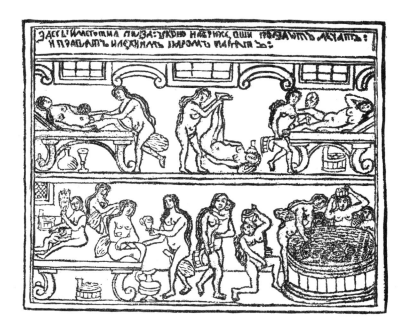

conception; and, of course, a look to the future and the possibilities of crossing that final frontier – sex in space.

It's a fact – in case you didn't know it – that a typical man and woman spend about 600 hours having sex between the ages of 20 and 70. It's also true that numbers of people are still remarkably ignorant about sexual matters, which helps to explain, of course, why so many thousands of sex manuals have been written over the years and what little good a lot of them have done. Which just happens to remind me of a couple of cautionary stories. The first is told by E.L. Parker in *Pilot Papers* (1947):

> A husband, realising that his part in copulation was deficient in skill, bought a number of manuals on sex education for marriage. Unfortunately, he failed to impart any of his newly acquired knowledge to his wife before coition, so she continued to maintain the reserve which was customary and the maladjustment persisted.

The second is a cutting from the *Glasgow Evening Times* of 12 October 1954:

> The Reverend Doctor John Quillan said it was with horror that he looked on the very thought of sex education in schools. 'Sex education,' he declared, 'resulted in the fall of the Roman Empire.'

Doctor Quillan would obviously not have found much favour with Heliogabalus – whose favourite punishment for those who displeased him was castration!

It is equally true to say that the 'advice' gathered in this book would have just about as much effect if put into practice. Indeed, it is clear that until the present century, sexual conduct has been moulded as far as its public image is concerned by folklore, dogma and private anxiety. Together with illness, it is the area where ideas of guilt, reparation and the forbidden are most evident – and, of course, it spills over into the field of hygiene, as it were, in its own right.

THE STRANGE EX-
OTIC WORLD OF
TWILIGHT MEN
AND WOMEN

THE THIRD SEX!
MAN OR WOMAN?
CAN YOU TELL
THEM FROM
OTHERS?.

MYSTERIOUS FASCINATION ··

A Great Social Evil Uncovered

Now a Doctor has dared to tear away the veil of mystery that hides the facts behind homosexuality. In blunt understandable words he describes the unbelievable facts. "STRANGE LOVES, A Study in Sexual Abnormalities," by Dr. La Forest Potter, noted authority, is a document so weird, so startling, as to amaze the civilized world. Dr. Potter says, "NO MAN ON EARTH HAS A CHANCE AGAINST A WOMAN ONCE SHE HAS SUCCUMBED TO ANOTHER WOMAN." A startling, provocative indictment against the false modesty that has been responsible for the growth of these fantastic strange amatory curiosities among savage and civilized races.

For hundreds of years men and women have talked with hushed voices about "STRANGE PEO-PLE"—men who are not men—women who are not women. No one has ever *dared* to talk out in the open about THE THIRD SEX. Is it any wonder that the shocking, lurid facts of this great social evil are unknown to the great mass of men and women. Because this subject is considered taboo, strange nick-names have arisen. "Fairies, Pansies, Queers, Lesbians, Perverts"—these are but a few of the names used to describe these *female men* and *male women*.

Dr. Potter tells about the hidden secret passions that dominate these women's exotic lives. He talks about the tragic duality of the effeminate man—half man —half woman. Fearlessly, openly, the meaning of many misunderstood subjects is brought under the searchlight of truth. Sadism — Necrophilia — Phallic Worship — Sodomy — Pederasty—Tribadism—Saphism—Uranism—the normal man and woman will refuse to believe that such abnormalities exist and have been practiced through the ages.

ASTONISHING DISCLOSURES ABOUT THE WORLD'S MOST FAMOUS MEN?

How many of the famous men of history were considered "odd"? Socrates, Plato, Caesar, Virgil, Oscar Wilde, Leonardo da Vinci, Lord Byron, Tchaikowsky, the musician; Walt Whitman, the gentle lovable poet; Napoleon—men and women of all kinds in all stages of life.

For Sophisticated Adult Readers!

This document in book form contains bewildering disclosures and discoveries of a subject that is seldom if ever discussed, that most people know little or nothing about—yet one that deserves the most painstaking and thorough investigation. A limited edition has been prepared for ADULTS ONLY. 256 pages, beautifully bound in cloth, printed on fine paper—for the book lover and collector of rare, esoteric literature. Reserve a copy of this book—the most startling document of its kind—by mailing the coupon.

ROBERT DODSLEY CO.
110 W. 42nd St., Dept. B-24, New York, N. Y.

THE ROBERT DODSLEY CO., Dept. B-24
110 West 42nd Street,
New York, N. Y.

Please send me IN PLAIN WRAPPER a copy of the original edition of Dr. La Forest Potter's book "STRANGE LOVES—A Study In Sexual Abnormalities." I hereby affirm that I am an adult person.
☐ I am enclosing remittance of $2.50. Send book all charges postpaid.
☐ Ship C. O. D. I promise to pay postman $2.50 plus postage on delivery.

Name ....

Address ....

Town................................ State...............
(We reserve the right to return all orders after this edition is exhausted. Prepaid orders receive preference and will be shipped before C. O. D. orders.) (Canadian and Foreign orders must be accompanied by remittance for $2.75.)

There have been many attempts made to understand and perfect the act of sex, as these pages bear witness. James Douglas, writing in the *Sunday Express* back in the thirties, may have thought he had the answer, but somehow makes the whole thing sound ridiculous. 'If only,' he wrote, 'men could love each other like dogs, the world would be a paradise.'

It is probably Alex Comfort, the noted historian of sex and sexual matters, who has come closest to putting the whole business into the right perspective when he wrote the following lines some years ago:

> Sex is a body-contact sport. It is safe to watch, but more fun to play. Although sex is a risky game, one is supposed to pretend that it is not. Yet it is the dangerousness, rather than the mysteriousness of the game, that provides sex 'experts' with their many followers. Promising to teach people how to play the sex game well, sexologists seduce them into believing that they can teach them how to play it safely – which, of course, no one can do.

I invite the reader, then, to be informed, instructed and no doubt amused by two centuries of the words of these 'teachers', their 'seductive' theories and, especially, the fallacies and fads to which they gave birth. And do bear in mind as you read that old saying, 'A myth is as good as a male', and some apt words by the poet George Barker in his *True Confession*:

> The act of human procreation,
> – O crown and flower, O admiration
> Of perfect love throughout creation,
> We are excreted, like shit.

1.

WOMEN ARE MEN TURNED OUTSIDE IN

RIDE TO RUMFORD

"Let the gall'd jade winch

The itinerant hawkers who toured the English countryside in the early eighteenth century selling all manner of goods including printed sheets of ballads and accounts of recent brutal murders had one very popular item for more broad-minded customers. It was an anonymous piece of verse which satirised the current state of scientific knowledge about men and women. The lines here are taken from a printing dated 1711, entitled *Women's Secrets Survey'd*:

Women's secrets I have survey'd,
And seen how curiously they're made,
And that, though they of different sexes be,
Yet on the whole they are the same as we.
For those that have the strictest searchers been,
Find women are but men turn'd outside in,
And men, if they but cast their eyes about,
May find they're women with their insides out.

So that's it. The secret of life, death and what makes men and women different. But you ain't seen nothing yet . . .

THE TURNING POINT

Ancient and medieval literature contains a number of stories about women who spread their legs so far apart that their organs fell out and they became men. Far-fetched as the idea may seem, some of the world's earliest physicians believed it to be true. Claudius Galen (c. AD 130–201), the Greek physician who is sometimes referred to as 'The Medical Pope' and was virtually the sole fountain of medical wisdom until the sixteenth century, certainly subscribed to the fallacy. Though he is credited with almost a hundred worthy treatises (including several commentaries on Hippocrates), was a careful dissector of animals and the first man to diagnose the human pulse, this is what he had to say about the sexes in *On the Usefulness of the Parts of the Body*:

> The female is more imperfect than the male. First, because she is the colder. And since among animals that one which is hotter is more perfect, so the colder must be more imperfect. The second proof of the imperfection of the female as compared with the male is seen when their bodies are dissected.
>
> Think first, please, of the man's sexual parts turned in and extending inward between the rectum and the bladder. If this should happen, the scrotum would necessarily take the place of the uteri, with the testes lying outside, next to it on either side. The penis of the male would become the neck of the cavity that had been formed; and the skin at the end of the penis, now called prepuce, would become the female pudendum itself. In fact, you could not find a single large male part left over that had not simply changed its position; for the parts that are inside in woman are outside in man . . .

THE SEAT OF LEARNING

Hippocrates (c. 460–359 BC) was undoubtedly the most celebrated physician of antiquity. Born on the Greek island of Cos where he also practised, he spent much of his life collecting all that he believed to be sound in the past history of medicine in order to write a series of influential works which were ultimately to include *Prognostica*, *De Morbis Popularibus* and *De Capitis Vulneribus*. Today, of course, his name lives on in the medical Hippocratic oath. For all his sobriety, though, Hippocrates could be unintentionally funny, as in his stern reproach to any woman who contemplated sex during pregnancy: 'Intercourse should be against the law at this time – as should walking upon hills, washing to excess and sitting upon soft cushions . . .'

THE WOMB WITH A VIEW

Aretaeus was a second-century Greek physician whose four books on the causes and symptoms of diseases rank him second only to Hippocrates. He was also something of a disciple of Galen and came up with a rather curious idea about the womb. It was rather like an animal, he declared, and tended to wander about inside women. How he reached this bizarre conclusion is quoted in *The Extant Works of Aretaeus the Cappadocian*:

> In the middle of the flanks of a woman lies the womb, a female viscus, closely resembling an animal – for it is moved of itself hither and thither in the flanks. It also moves upwards in a direct line to below the cartilage of the thorax, and obliquely to the right or to the left, either to the liver or spleen. Likewise it is subject to prolapsus downwards, and, in a word, is altogether erratic.

THE INSATIABLE WITCH

The early Christian Church's obsession with sex caused it to treat females as the source of all sexual evil. 'A good woman,' one (anonymous) medieval authority wrote, 'is but like one Ele put in a bagge amongst 500 Snakes, and if a man should have the luck to grope out that one Ele from all the Snakes, yet he hath at best but a wet Ele by the Taile.' Two Dominican priests, Jakob Sprenger (1436–95) and Heinrich Kramer (1430–1505), sent by Pope Innocent VIII to investigate witchcraft and demonology, produced a savage condemnation of the fair sex in their subsequent book, *Malleus Maleficarum* (Hammer of Witches), printed in 1486 and containing a host of material on demonology and black magic. In this they declared categorically that all witchcraft came from carnal lust, 'which in women is insatiable', and continued:

> All other wickedness is nothing compared to the wickedness of a woman. She is an enemy of friendship, an unavoidable punishment, a necessary evil, a natural temptation, a desirable calamity, an evil of nature, painted with pretty colours . . .
>
> She is more carnal than man, as is obvious from her many carnal abominations. It should be recalled that the first woman was defectively formed because she was made from a bent rib, the breast rib. Through this defect, she is an imperfect creature, always deceiving . . .
>
> A woman is beautiful to look upon, contaminating to the touch, and deadly to keep. Truly we may agree with Cato of Utica who says that if the world could be rid of women, we would not be without God . . .

THE BALD FACTS & OTHERS

Little changed as far as attitudes to sexual science were concerned for hundreds of years. Indeed, a seventeenth-century German physician, Kaspar Hofmann, still agreed with Galen's view that women were the inferior sex. A female, he said, was a 'naturally mutilated man'. In his book, *De Generatione Hominis*, which appeared in 1629, he offered a variety of opinions to support this view – of which the following are the most curious:

> A male child is produced when the semen is very well-concocted and the menses well-tempered. A female results from the interaction of cruder semen with excrementitious blood for, as Hippocrates says, both sexes have male and female semen.

> As affirmed by Hippocrates and Galen, a male is produced from semen from the right testicle which falls into the right horn of the uterus. The whole world knows that the right is superior to the left.

> A male grows quicker during its uterine life and slower afterwards. A female causes more physical trouble to the mother during gestation.

> The male can withstand heat and cold better. I do not speak of the woman's habit of standing for a long time in cold water washing, for woman becomes a semi-aquatic animal, as our Scherbius was wont to say facetiously.

> The male is more often ambidextrous and has larger veins.

> The excrement of a male child is less offensive to the sense of smell than the female. Thomas Erastus used to say that if ten women were sick in one place, it smelt worse than thirty men in another.

The male grows bald often owing to dryness due to his superior heat and is more animated, liberal, constant, open, like a lion. The female is fearful, greedy, always on the move, like a fox . . .

THE ETIQUETTE OF COITION

One of the earliest works to offer sexual etiquette to men and women was an inoffensively titled little book, *De Sancto Matrimonio*, which was first published in Spain during the early years of the sixteenth century. It was clearly intended only for married couples and the author, Thomas Sanchez (1550–1610), was a Jesuit and also the director of a school at Granada. In the main, he dealt with the legal, moral and religious questions of marriage, but in a section devoted to the positions for intercourse, he provided his readers – probably unconsciously – with an unequalled mixture of religious fervour and bawdy guidance, as these four extracts reveal:

> Coitus with the woman superincumbent is not only offensive to natural decency – since man should naturally be active and woman passive – but more gravely suspect still for the danger of preventing the peaceful possession of the vagina by the semen . . .

> It is a mortal sin for a husband and wife to have intercourse with the normal position reversed, because it makes the woman active, a mutation which, as anyone can see, nature must abhor. Furthermore, according to certain authorities, the Flood was caused by the vile custom of women mounting upon men in the sexual act . . .

> It is permissible under God's laws to commence love-making with anal entry provided that the act is concluded with vaginal sex . . .

> If, when engaged in sex with a whore, a man withdraws before

ejaculation, he is considered to have repented and not sinned against God's laws . . .

GENTLEMEN ALWAYS PREFERRED BLONDES

The year 1642 saw the publication of *Rare Verities, The Cabinet of Venus Unlock'd* by the Italian Giovanni Sinibaldi, which has been described as one of the most beautiful medical books – typographically – and the origin of 'very nearly all the major nonsense about reproduction and sexual matters generally which was to haunt counselling literature to the present day', according to historian Alex Comfort. Very little is known about the author beyond the facts he was born at Lionessa and became professor of medicine at Rome, where he wrote and published his sexual treatise under the title *Geneanthropeia*. (It was an opportunist London printer named Briggs 'at the Dolphin in St. Paul's Church-yard' who gave the book its familiar title when he translated it in 1658.) The book is a wonderful collection of facts and fallacies, in which Sinibaldi asks (and, in some cases, answers) questions about sex, makes observations on current knowledge, and hands out advice. Here are some typical extracts:

Question: What are the physiognomical signs of Lust?
Answer: A little straight forehead denotes an unbridled appetite in lust.

Question: What are the signs of Virginity?
Answer: Little ears demonstrate aptness to venery.

Question: Why do night pollutions afford more pleasure and do more to debilitate than a man's spontaneous copulation with a woman?
Answer: It is an infallible sign of this, if a man is bald and not old; but if old and not bald, you may conclude he hath lost one of his stones or both.

Sinibaldi's Mysteries of Sex:

* What was the sex life of Adam and Eve like?
* Did the Virgin Mary have a menstrual cycle?
* Could Nature more opportunely have located the male organ elsewhere?
* Why did Nature endow man with one penis and not two?
* Would reproduction be better served by a process of vegetation instead of coition?

Sinibaldi's Facts of Sex:

The seat of female pleasure is in the clitoris – Realdus Columbus (1593) claims to have discovered it and marvelled that so many noted anatomists overlooked so pretty and useful a thing.

The seat of male pleasure is the foreskin, but we should enquire why this structure so greatly enhances female pleasure? I ask my readers not to treat this question as trifling or ridiculous, for the Jewish women, Turkesses and Mauritaniae, their husbands being shorn, made much of it, and most gladly accepted the embraces of Christians (so it is said).

All women are lascivious, but auburn blondes the most.

A sad or weeping woman cannot conceive.

Experience tells us that Virgins ravished are never with child; or, on the other side, if she be possessed with too much joy.

Sinibaldi's Better Sex Guide:

Sex is good for the phlegm, for epilepsy, depression, mental patients and green-sick virgins . . .

Cold feet are a powerful hindrance to coition – couples should wear soft, noiseless slippers . . .

Aphrodisiacs are recommended. The best are rest, boredom, sleep, red meat – followed by wine, prosperity, fun, music and pleasant surroundings . . .

Flogging is good for people. What pleasure can come from pain, sweetness from bitter, lust from bloody wounds!

Finally, it is probably as well to draw a veil over Sinibaldi's final two pieces of advice:

How To Shorten the Yard, Being Too Long

How To Enlarge the Pudenda, Being Too Small

THE OBSERVANCE OF VENUS

In France, the country so long associated with the finer points of love-making, the best-selling sex manual for generations was *Tableau de l'Amour Conjugal* by Nicolas Venette (1633–98), first published in 1686. This apparently went into over thirty editions during the eighteenth century and was translated into most of the European languages. Venette studied medicine in Paris, travelled widely in Italy and Portugal, and published his first book – a treatise on scurvy – in 1671. Before getting down to the serious business of human sexuality, he also wrote on subjects as diverse as nightingales, pruning fruit trees and the treatment of water supplies. He first issued *Tableau de l'Amour* in Amsterdam under the anagram 'Salocini, Venetien' and the work is a mixture of erotica and ribaldry which delighted – if not necessarily informed – its countless readers. Among his finer points of guidance are the following:

It would be as well for couples to inspect each other's reproductive equipment . . .

Nothing is more certain than that unbounded licentiousness in the conduct of the marriage bed is the ruin of many thousands of couples . . .

It has long been so that the normal position for intercourse is *Venus observata* (the 'missionary position'). But *More canino* ('doggy fashion') has much to be said for it, being easier, not least, for fat men and pregnant women . . .

In those circumstances where the penis is too long for the woman's comfort, a cork ring may be slipped upon the organ, though I have heard few complaints of this of late . . .

The best aphrodisiacs are opium, bengue [hashish] and betel, though these are aids to marriage and should not be misused by libertines. Perhaps the best of all is water, for Venus herself was born upon the ocean . . .

Forbear the mercenary harlot, and think of the joys that await you in the arms of a mistress or a wife . . .

Horse riding is the best cure for impotence . . .

THE FIELDWORK OF THE CHINESE

For centuries, very little was known in the West about the sexual life of the people in the closed-off world of China. In fact, the Chinese had long before evolved their own particular attitude to sex, as is revealed in a three-volume work known as the *So Nu Ning* assembled in AD 618. A collection of sexual lore and techniques, it showed that sex was considered a natural expression and emotional and sentimental attachments had nothing to do with it. Marriage was for producing children and no man was expected to be faithful to his wife. Here are eight of the more curious directives to be found in the pages of the *So Nu Ning*:

The basic aim for the male is to conserve as much as possible his seminal essence . . .

During intercourse, the man's body is nourished by the orgasm of the female and strengthened by the retention of his own sperm . . .

Intercourse with girls from fourteen to eighteen gives the man greater energy, while a woman of thirty or over has little essence left . . .

Acts of intercourse with a succession of partners strengthen a man's vital powers . . .

Orgasm is to be avoided and permitted only when children are desired . . .

To overcome ejaculation, the man should press a finger on the urethra between the scrotum and the anus and cause the sperm to ascend in his body and nourish his brain . . .

The proper technique for sex is one time deep and nine times shallow . . .

Sex once in a field or along the roadside is equal to a thousand times in bed . . .

A MASTERPIECE OF SEX

Probably the most famous – and certainly most widely reprinted – sex manual of the eighteenth and nineteenth century was *Aristotle's Masterpiece*, accredited to the famous Greek philosopher and scientist, but almost certainly the work of several later anonymous writers. The book was first known to be circulating in a Latin edition in the Middle Ages and subsequently proved to be particularly popular in colonial America. Copies continued to be sold in sex shops on both sides of the Atlantic until well into this century. Here are a selection of the *Masterpiece*'s more amusing observations:

ON SEXUAL PLEASURE:
Women are never better pleased when they are often satisfied by intercourse, which pleasure and delight is affirmed is double in women to what it is in men. For as the delight of men consists chiefly in the ejection of seed, so women are delighted both by the ejection of their own [seed] and the reception of the man's.

ON THE SEX OF CHILDREN:

If a male child is to be produced, then in the coition, the woman must lie on her right flank, because boys are engendered on the right side of the womb. Intercourse when the moon is on the wane will produce a female child.

ON TESTS FOR CONCEPTION:

If the urine of the woman be put in a glass three days and she has conceived, certain live things will appear to stir in it.

If a bright needle be put in a whole night and she has conceived, divers little red Specks will be thereon, but if not it will be blackish or rusty.

ON ADULTERY:

If women allow their fancies to drift during coition, they may produce a deformity or even a hybrid man-beast.

And, if in the act of copulation, the woman earnestly looks on the man, and fixes her mind on him, the child will resemble his father. Nay, if a woman, even in unlawful copulation, fix her mind upon her husband, the child will resemble him though he did not beget it.

ON BREASTS:

If it is a male child, the right breast swells first, the right eye is brighter than the left, the face is high-coloured, because the colour is such as the blood is, and as the male is conceived of purer blood and of more perfect seed than the female.

ON ERECTIONS:

Erection is chiefly caused by cresses, crysmon, parsnips, artichokes, turnips, asparagus, sea shell fish, candied ginger and acorns bruised to powder and drunk in muscadel . . .

ON VIRGINITY:

When a man is married and finds the tokens of his wife's virginity upon the first copulation, he has all the reason in the world to believe her such, and to rest satisfied that he has married a virgin. But if on the contrary, he finds her not, then he has no reason to think her devirginated, if he finds her otherwise sober and modest.

ON LIFESTYLES:
City women that live high and do very little by way of exercise, seldom have children.

WHEN THERE IS NO FEELING . . .

A feature of many nineteenth-century sex manuals was a belief by the authors that women of the time – unlike their sisters in the Middle Ages – had no feelings about sex and most were completely passive throughout coition. Among these writers was William Acton (1813–75), a clergyman's son from Dorset who became an apothecary in London, an expert on female venereal diseases, and then devoted years of his life to a first-hand investigation of prostitution. Among his many books and essays – both medical and popular – the following curious extract is taken from *A Practical Treatise in Diseases of the Urinary and Generative Organs in Both Sexes*, published in 1841, in which he explains his conviction about the sexual nature of women and evidently seeks to reassure any inadequate young man who might be reading:

I have taken pains to obtain and compare abundant evidence on this subject, and the result of my inquiries I may briefly epitomize as follows – I should say that the majority of women (happily for society) are not very much troubled with sexual feeling of any kind. As a general rule, a modest woman seldom desires any sexual gratification for herself. She submits to her husband's embraces, but principally to gratify him: and, were it not for the desires of maternity, would far rather be relieved from his attentions. No nervous or feeble young man, need, therefore, be deterred from marriage by any exaggerated notion of the arduous duties required from him.

THE GRAPES OF WRATH

Despite its rather prosaic title, *The Requirements of Motherhood* (1858) was actually a deliberately intimidating book. It was the work of a French physician with the singularly inappropriate name of Dr G.H. Naphey, who was also something of a religious fanatic and pulled no punches in warning his readers of the dangers that awaited them if and when they became pregnant. Three examples from the work will illustrate its mixture of the comic and the terrifying:

> What of children born to women who have been married previously? They will suffer through the operation of a mysterious and inexorable law for the sins not committed by its own father, but by the first husband of its mother . . .

> Is intercourse during pregnancy really dangerous? Yes, and particularly for the offspring. Mark these facts: If a pregnant woman willingly indulges even though loathing the act, she impresses sexual loathing and disgust on the child. This completely spoils daughters as wives . . .

> Do a pregnant mother's experiences affect the offspring? Indeed they do. I know of the case of a pregnant lady who saw some grapes, longed intensely for them, and constantly thought of them. During her period of gestation she was attacked and much alarmed by a turkey-cock. In due course, she gave birth to a child having a large cluster of globular tumours growing from the tongue and exactly resembling our common grapes. And on the child's chest there grew a red excrescence exactly resembling a turkey's wattles . . .

RIGHT LEG OVER FOR A BOY

A German physician, Dr Albert Sixt, startled the medical profession of his country in 1860 with a paper entitled *The Theory of Testicles*, which also became something of a *cause célèbre* in the national press. In this little work he claimed that during sex, the sperm was actually ejected from only *one* of the testicles: if it came from the right one then a boy would result; from the left, a girl. Sixt said that the husband who wanted to be sure of getting a boy should have coition just before his wife's period. The chances of success could be doubled if the bed was correctly aligned with the compass and the moon was in its correct phase – though he neglected to explain what these might be. The doctor's instructions added:

> If a boy is to be generated, the husband must lie to the right of his wife and put the right knee over first, thus producing tension, which draws up the right testicle into place. If, however, the left testicle should somehow become drawn up towards the abdomen, it may be pushed down quite easily, during coition, and the right one pushed up to be sure of attaining the desired end.

BEATING THE WIND WITH YOUR FIST

Mrs Elisabeth Osgood Goodrich Willard was an American lady with a mission. Although without any medical training, she wrote a very popular pseudo-sex manual, *Sexology as the Philosophy of Life* (1867), in which she described an orgasm as 'more debilitating than a whole day's work'. She also compared regular sexual activity in the curious terminology of being like 'a man beating the wind with his fist' and added for good measure:

> It is this constant abuse of the sexual organs, producing constant failures and the most loathsome diseases; it is this ridiculous farce of a strong man putting forth all the nervous energy of his system, till he is perfectly prostrated by the effort, without one worthy motive, purpose or end; it is this which has so disgraced the act of impregnation. When human beings are generated under such conditions, it is no wonder they go through life as criminals, without a single good purpose or deed, and where all sense of shame is not lost, hanging their heads as if ashamed of their existence . . .

MALE, FEMALE AND URNING

A claim that at a certain stage of development both male and female were the same was put forward in 1869 by a German writer, Karl Heinrich Ulrichs, in a book entitled *Memnon* which he signed with the curious pen-name 'Numa Numantius'. The sexes remained the same, he said, until a threefold division took place into male, female and *urning*. 'Numa Numantius' explained:

> The urning, or urningin, has the physical features of one sex, but an inversion of love object since the sexual instinct does not correspond to his or her sexual organs. Thus it is natural

for some individuals to prefer their own sex rather than the opposite sex, and the danger for these people in their sexual activities is no greater than between a man and wife and no more unnatural.

What the inhibited old German meant by this euphemism was 'homosexuality' – a word that had actually already been coined by a fellow countryman, Karoly Maria Benkert, in *Des Preuszischen Strafgesetbuches* in April 1851.

THE SOTADIC ZONE

During the later part of the nineteenth century – and even well into the twentieth – there was a great deal of 'pseudo-scientific' writing on the subject of homosexuality. Much of it was the work of cranks – particularly in Germany which seems to have had a larger share of such people than any other country – and the books have been rightly dismissed in the same way as the literature of racism. Most of the writers were violently prejudiced and regarded homosexuality as 'a form of evil degeneracy'. In his book *Fads and Fallacies in the Name of Science* (1952), Martin Gardner has this to say about such volumes:

> Eccentric theories of homosexuality range all the way from those of the occultists who think a male soul becomes incarnated in a female body, or vice versa, to more scientific authorities who find 'homosexual centres' in the brain. The American writer, Charles G. Leland, produced a curious book in 1904, *The Alternate Sex*, which argued that the subconscious mind was always of the opposite gender. Leland had frequent dreams in which he imagined he was a woman, and from this made his generalisation. One of the strangest of all homosexual theories was advanced by the English explorer, Sir Richard Burton. He thought there was a geographical strip circling the globe, called the 'Sotadic Zone', in which inversion was concentrated . . .

THE ELECTRICITY OF SEX

Professor Orson Squire Fowler was a Victorian scientist who came to the conclusion that human beings were driven by their own kind of electricity – men being always positive and women negative. After half a century of study, he published *Sexual Science* in 1870, in which he claimed that 'the parent who casts the gender originates the opposite sex'. In other words, it was an update of the long-held belief that very masculine men have most daughters while very feminine women conceive more boys. Among the other theories that Fowler offered were several which defied logic or kept his options fully open:

* The first parent to reach orgasm will thereby cause the child to have the opposite sex . . .
* The parent with more 'vital force' will determine the child's sex . . .
* Twins and triplets undoubtedly originate in second and third copulations, immediately following the first, each drawing and then impregnating an egg. The fact that twins are born as soon as possible after each other supports this view . . .
* Neglect or crossness deadens a wife's love and thereby shrivels her mammaries . . .

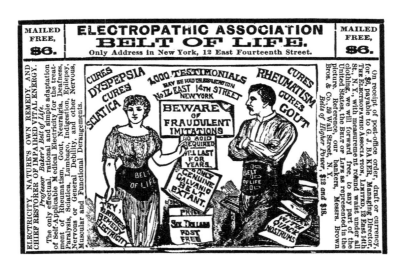

THE WHOLE WORLD A BROTHEL

The publication in 1886 of *Psychopathia Sexualis* by Richard Krafft-Ebing (1840–1902), a German specialist in nervous diseases, created a sensation. The book set out to prove that every kind of sexual activity except that leading to procreation was a psychopathic act and in so doing cited over 200 cases of 'abnormal' or 'pathological' men and women. Yet in the same groupings with lust murderers and cannibals, Krafft-Ebing included such harmless phenomena as a collector of violet-striped handkerchiefs, a man who loved to smell roses and a girl who longed to kiss and embrace other girls. Despite the fact that the text was liberally sprinkled with Latin words to make the more lurid passages acceptable, the mixture of fallacies and frauds sold in vast quantities to the general public and was 'sometimes regarded as the scientific last word by those who should know better', according to most experts. Although it has been argued that Krafft-Ebing 'blazed a path which other modern sexologists would follow' – though discarding most of his conclusions – some of his comments verge on the outrageous:

> Rampant sexuality despoils the unfolding bud of perfume and beauty, and leaves behind only the coarse, animal desire for sexual satisfaction. The glow of sensual sensibility wanes, and the inclination toward the opposite sex is weakened . . .

> If a woman is normally developed mentally and well-bred, her sexual desire is small. If this were not so, the whole world would become a brothel and marriage and a family impossible . . .

VICE AND VERSA

Nobody is ever entirely male or female, according to Otto Weininger (1882–1903), a feverishly enthusiastic young sexologist and author of *Sex and Character* (1903), for a time one of the most notorious sex manuals of the early twentieth century. Weininger said he had reached his conclusions from 'laboratory experiments [sic] and introspective analysis', though his book immediately split the medical profession and general public into two camps: those who thought him a crank and others – notably extreme feminists – who believed him a genius who had 'brilliantly applied algebraic formulae for the different types of men and women'. Whichever side you were on, poor Weininger, who had written the book when he was just twenty-one, was not around to experience the furore. He committed suicide before the first copies even reached the shops. He explained his philosophy in these words:

> Sexual attraction, in my view, most strongly exists between beings having complementary proportions of male and female, thus making up a complete person of each . . . Far from being separate but equal, or having different but equally valuable functions, the sexes – in ideal and unmixed form – are totally different, the male positive, the female negative. Woman is nothing but sexuality, she is sexuality itself, and falls into two classes: the maternal type and the prostitute.

THE BATTLE OF THE SEXES

During all the upheaval of the First World War, a London zoologist named Walter Heape came to the conclusion that men and women were not only completely different physically – surprise, surprise! – but the differences between their objectives in life had actually existed since the very earliest times. Therefore, he argued, their sexual needs were completely different, too, and the concept of monogamy could only generate what he called *Sex Antagonism*, which he took for the title of his book, published in 1913. In it he wrote:

> Rigid societal laws of sexual conduct favour the growth of drastic sex antagonism as society becomes more and more

complicated and the life of people becomes more purely artificial. By their pernicious constraint upon natural tendencies, the present sex laws weigh as heavily, if not much more heavily on men, and I have found as remarkable, complacency of the dissatisfied man. Sex antagonism due to the neglect of Nature's laws has led some women, undoubtedly spinsters, exhibiting the type of mental derangement associated with degeneration of the functional capacity of the generative, into vociferous opposition to the existing state of affairs. In my view, women would be better advised to cultivate dominant female qualities and by increasing their value, they will gain power which no man can usurp.

A WORLD OF TWO HALVES

Arabella Kenealy made a reputation for herself in the early years of the twentieth century as a fervent opponent of feminism. She also dedicated her life to proving a theory that the entire world – and the cosmos beyond – was half male and half female. She explained all in a curious book, *The Human Gyroscope*, published in 1934, which was subtitled 'A Consideration of the Gyroscopic Rotation of Earth as a Mechanism of the Evolution of Terrestrial Living Forms, Explaining the Phenomenon of Sex: its Origin and Development and its Significance in the Evolutionary Process'. The very first sentence in the book stating Mrs Kenealy's thesis hardly allowed the reader to draw breath, let alone a conclusion:

> In presenting the consideration that, as plastic clay on the rotary disc of the little potter's wheel of industry is shapen and moulded in varieties of symmetrical three-dimensional form, increasingly uprising in the vertical, so upon the rotating surface of the great terrestrial potter's wheel of Creative Evolution, the plastic matter of terrestrial organisms has been shapen and moulded in the countless diversities of increasingly complex, structurally differentiated three-dimensional forms of living species, progressively uprising in the vertical in the terms of increasingly complex elevated posture – I have ventured to base my argument upon the Gravitation of great Newton, instead of on the later Einstein theory.

The main points of the book were:

1. The Cosmos exhibits a dual male-female aspect from the lowly atom to the lofty galaxy.
2. Maleness and femaleness are, in fact, the warp and weft of the fabric of creation.
3. The northern races of our world are masculine, while those in the south are feminine owing to the Earth's rotary movements.
4. The right side of every human being is more masculine than the left.

MURDER IS TOO GOOD!

The advice columns about matters of sex and sexuality in women's magazines have been a tradition in Britain, America and many other parts of the world for much of this century. A US publication, *Secret Loves*, probably enjoys the record for having handed out some of the most amusing admonitions to its female readers. These five typical examples are taken from issues in the fifties:

> Any man who loves a woman other than his invalided, shrewish wife may well be suspected of murdering this wife when she finally dies . . .

> A single girl and a married man who are desperately in love with each other have no right to exchange a single kiss . . .

> The man who so much as kisses a girl other than his wife is a cheap, unfaithful cheat and is only fit to be horsewhipped . . .

> A married woman who commits adultery because her husband is a hopeless cripple deserves to die a horrible death . . .

> Any man who, in an explosive burst of temper, kills his wife's paramour, should unquestionably be acquitted under the unwritten law . . .

NEVER MAKE LOVE TO A WOMAN WITH BIG HANDS . . .

Superstition has played a major role in the development of quite a number of sex fallacies, as the reader will probably already have begun to appreciate. Despite their obvious origin in folklore, some of these curious ideas about lovers and love-making are still current in parts of the world today. In her wide-ranging book *A Dictionary of Omens and Superstitions*, first published in 1978 and subsequently reprinted several times, Philippa Waring devotes a section to 'Sex' in which the following segment is particularly relevant:

Perhaps the most widely quoted of all such ideas is that men with large hands have big penises, while a woman with a generous mouth is sure to have a large vagina. Equally wide-spread is a belief that Latin men and those from hot countries have more sexual potency because of the generative power of the sun. Similarly, men whose bodies are covered in hair are more vital than those who are not. To such superstitions can be added the idea that too much sex weakens the heart and can lead to blindness, just as masturbation is harmful.

Interestingly, to these still-current old myths have been added some peculiarly modern superstitions: such as sun lamps arouse sexual passion, girls with contact lenses cannot take oral contraceptive pills, and the wedding ceremony confers immunity from catching venereal disease! America, in particular, has become the centre of some ever stranger sex superstitions. For example, blondes are said to be dumb, but much more eager for sex than brunettes – although redheads have a greater enthusiasm than either. Among men it is claimed that sex during a woman's period can lead to baldness, even impotence. And girls have an idea that a cola douche will prevent pregnancy – apparently a modern variation on the old idea of taking a hot bath topped up with lashings of gin . . .

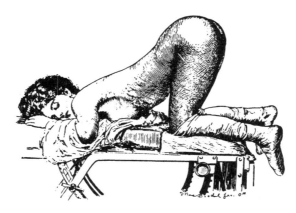

RED MEAT FOR A BOY!

Hearing a claim in one of the southern states of America that the sex of a child was caused by whether the man or the woman made love more vigorously – thereby determining the gender – prompted sexologist Dr Landrum B. Shettles to conduct his own survey in 1979 to discover if there were similar examples of this girls-making-boys tradition. His research extended around the world and revealed there was, indeed, a whole variety of such 'interesting if unproven theories'. Here are six of the most amusing examples:

* In several Western countries, eating lots of cakes and sweets before sex will produce a girl; lots of red meat is required for a boy . . .
* Women in the Palau Islands in the Pacific who want a male child dress up in men's clothes before having sex . . .
* From Germany came the idea that a husband should take an axe to bed and sing a catchy tune to ensure an heir . . .
* In Romania, a bride will allow a small boy to step on her hands before going on honeymoon if she wants a male child . . .
* Several of the African nations observe a long-standing tradition which involves men drinking a mixture of wine and lion's blood before having sex . . .
* And in a number of rural districts of Britain, there are still those who believe that a woman should be facing south during love-making to get a boy . . .

THE RECIPROCITY OF AMORANT FEELINGS

Many writers and poets have tried to define sexual love – but it takes scientists to come up with perhaps the most bizarre, virtually incomprehensible, definition. In September 1977, the first International Conference on Love and Attraction was held in Wales at Swansea and was attended by some two hundred psychologists from twelve countries. After hearing talks on subjects as diverse as 'Seductive Behaviour in Hospitalized Persons' and 'Personality Characteristics of the Average Rubber Fetishist', the assembly put its collective heads together to find a definition for what makes the world go round. This is what the boffins came up with after three days of deliberation: 'Love is the cognitive-affective state characterized by intrusive and obsessive fantasizing concerning reprocity and amorant feeling by the object of amorance, or OA.'

But enough of jargon. Let's get on with the next section of fallacies and fads of sex . . .

2.

PENIS PRIDE AND VESTAL VIRGINS

LYSISTRATA.

The one physical aspect of his body that puzzled primitive man the most was his penis. Research into the lives of prehistoric tribes has revealed that some of them believed their genitals hardly belonged to them at all. They were either a devil, an animal that had attached itself to them or, worst of all, a predatory parasite. The only thing that made life bearable with a penis was special medicine or ritual magic. In his book *Sex, Sin and Sanctity* (1954), John Langdon-Davis cites the example of the Ba-Ila people of Rhodesia whose ideas typified early man's apprehension about this mysterious accoutrement . . .

They believed that the sexual organs were animals, or at least the dwelling-places of animals, called *bapuka*, which controlled them and were responsible for the process of reproduction. It is a *mupuka* in the male that secretes the semen, and impotence is caused by its ceasing to function. It is thought that hens' eggs, fat and a dish of ground-nuts will prevent the *mupuka* from working or, by becoming fixed in the loins, will block the passage.

In a woman there are said to be two of these *bapuka*, one male, the other female. The male is the inert creature, but upon the female depend all the generative functions. The name given to this female *mupuka* is *Chibumba*, the moulder. It is so named because it forms the child in the womb. It lies within the uterus, with its head in the orifice. When in coitus, the semen reaches it, the *Chibumba* catches it in its mouth. Having secured the semen, it licks and rolls it over and over and this way forms it into a foetus.

Try explaining all *that* as the facts of life!

PENIS PRIDE

The pioneer Greek physician, Claudius Galen, has also been called 'one of the most articulate exponents history has ever known of "Penis Pride".' His eulogy on the design and functions of the male organ occupies no fewer than three entire chapters in his great treatise on human sexuality. He believes the penis to be 'perfectly positioned' and asks:

> For where else could you transport the male penis? Nearer the behind than at present? But then it will cause annoyance in the act of defecation, unless you think it better that the member be always in erection? If thereby it does not cause annoyance in the act of defecation, it becomes a life-long embarrassment . . .
>
> Perhaps it were preferable to place it higher on the pubis? Tell me also if in that position it is always to be erect, or always flaccid? If always in erection, apart from its being exposed, it would be an annoyance all the rest of the time and only useful in coitus. Were it perpetually flaccid, it would be completely useless and unable to fulfil the function for which it was created.

Game, set and love match.

THE SIZE OF A CROCODILE

The ancient Egyptians had no doubts that the penis was in the right position. But size was all-important to the men of the Nile and there are ancient documents which show that they went to considerable lengths to enlarge the penis in order to enhance sexual pleasure. These varied from placing animal bones inside the foreskin to ritual sacrifice to the gods. One old papyrus scroll revealed the strangest of all: 'To enlarge the penis, regularly rub with crocodile droppings.'

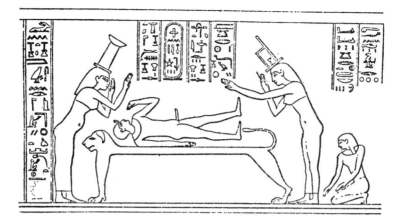

TAKE ONE WILD ASS

The Roman naturalist Pliny the Elder (AD 23–79) spent a lot of time at war and wrote a treatise on the throwing of missiles from horseback before turning his attention to the world of nature and compiling his masterwork, *Historia Naturalis* (AD 77). In this he took a leaf out of ancient Egyptian philosophy and declared his belief in the healing powers of urine and dung for sexual problems, especially to do with the genitals. Among his many observations will be found the following:

> Any diseases of the penis are best treated by the application upon it of wild ass's urine . . .

> The man who urinates where a dog has previously made water will be susceptible to numbness in his loins and find his member difficult to raise . . .

> The dung of hens will cure impotence in a man . . .

What a way to revive the old cock-a-doodle-do!

'AN UNRULY CREATURE'

It would have been a surprise if the great Greek philosopher Plato (c.427–347 BC) had not given a thought or two to male and female genitals: after all, there was not much else of the human body and psyche that escaped his attention. A much-travelled man who loved life and died at a wedding feast when he was eighty-one, he had this to say in his famous dialogue, *Timaeus*:

> . . . And so it came about that the gods contrived the love of sexual intercourse by constructing an animate creature of one kind in us men, and of another kind in women. Wherefore in men the nature of the genital organs is disobedient and self-willed, like a creature that is deaf to reason, and it attempts to dominate all because of its frenzied lusts. And in women again, owing to the same causes, whenever the matrix or the womb, as it is called – which is an indwelling creature desirous of child-bearing – remains without fruit long beyond the due season, it is vexed and takes ill; and by straying all ways through the body and blocking up the passages of the breath and preventing respiration it casts the body into the uttermost distress, and causes, moreover, all kinds of maladies; until the desire and love of the two sexes unite them.

So it's Plato we have to blame for that old line about a standing dick having no conscience?

THE WELL-GROWN MEMBER

The sixteenth-century medical writer Gabriele Falloppio was big on private parts in his little work about surgery and physiology, *De Decoratione*. Towards the end of the 56-page volume, he urged the parents of small boys to pay particular attention to the genitals of their offspring: 'I urge you to take every pain in infancy to enlarge the privy member of boys by massaging, and the application of stimulants, since a well-grown specimen never comes amiss . . .'

Falloppio also agreed with a current view that it was disgraceful for any man to reveal his uncovered glans to a woman – or anyone else for that matter. It was worse than being naked. 'Should it be asked why Almighty God ordained that his chosen people should do away with their foreskins, the reasons are eternal and laid up in the mind of the Almighty, and must not be recounted in profane schools . . .'

Perhaps it was to keep the minds of the Jews off sex and on religion, maybe?

BREWER'S DROOP

William Shakespeare (1564–1616) lived a rumbustious life in between writing some of the greatest plays and poetry in the English language. His tales of love and violence, his word pictures of men and women lusting and drinking, reflect both his own life and that of his contemporaries. He loved a glass or two, did Will, and may well have suffered from time to time the familiar complaint known as 'Brewer's Droop' – certainly we have the evidence of the porter in *Macbeth* who says with wry insight of the demon drink that 'it provokes the desire, but takes away the performance'. Clement Freud, the politician, writer and former professional cook, amusingly describes a couple of (alleged) remedies for this condition in his book *Hangovers* (1981):

> The classic remedy is to burn together the liver of a frog and a
> hedgehog, place the ashes in a bag and carry this around the

person so as not to be embarrassed by impotence at awkward moments. By the late 18th century, due to one thing and another, including the national shortage of hedgehogs, strychnine was offered as a substitute. This can be effective, provided that you bear in mind that a little strychnine goes a long way and a lot lands you at the Assizes on a charge of rape.

DROPPED OFF!

Attitudes towards the male sex organ have, of course, been many and varied – but few more outlandish than this one expressed in an editorial in *The Church Militant* published in London in 1949: 'In the future when man learns to control his disordered impulses, the time will come when the sex organs will atrophy and disappear. Man will then produce his kind from his larynx which will be transformed to speak the Creative Word. Meanwhile, we must make the best of a bad job.'

WHY ONE HANGS LOWER

An extraordinary little booklet, *The New Morality*, published anonymously in New York in 1909, devoted considerable space to extolling the virtues of the testicles. 'See the matchless Mind and Hand of the Creator in these extremely necessary glands,' the unknown author wrote, and then continued:

> The testes are located *on the outside of the body*. Did you ever wonder WHY? The Creator had a very good reason. This will be explained.
>
> Many men themselves do not realise it, but the left testicle hangs a little lower in the scrotum than the right. There is an important *reason*. Could blind evolution without intelligence have thought this out and made it thus?
>
> There is perhaps no pain a boy or man can suffer that is as excruciating as a crushing or injury to the testicles. Did 'blind' nature know this? Or did an All-intelligent Creator, concerned for our welfare, design it so that, in case the thighs are crowded together, one testicle will slip over the other, thus avoiding any crushing. No evolution here!

THE FAMILY JEWELS

Often referred to as the 'Family Jewels', testicles were held in special esteem in the Middle East a thousand years ago. Indeed, women had to take care not to injure their menfolk's genitals when making love – or the law would punish them severely, as these lines from an Assyrian document of the second century BC make only too clear:

> If a woman has crushed a man's testicles while involved in coition, then one of her fingers shall be cut off.
>
> If the other testicle becomes affected along with it by catching the infection, even though a physician has bound it up, or she

has crushed the other testicle during coition, they shall tear out both her eyes.

A case of keeping your eye on the balls, girls.

ANOTHER BALLS-UP

A justifiably famous newspaper headline published in the fifties described the uncertainty surrounding a charity event that was to be hosted by the leading civic dignitary of a London suburb. It read: MAYOR'S BALL HANGS IN BALANCE. However, one of our greatest writers, Jane Austen (1775–1817), probably inadvertently started this whole tradition of literary balls-ups back in 1811 when she published *Sense and Sensibility*, for in it she wrote: 'In winter his private balls were numerous enough to any young lady who was not suffering under the insatiable appetite of fifteen.'

A HAMMER BLOW

The ancient Chinese are believed to have been the first people to have gone in for penis enlargement. Some very early accounts describe physicians attaching weights to small organs in order to lengthen the size, while in one of the country's classic erotic novels, *The Before-Midnight Scholar*, there is a lurid description of a process whereby a quartered dog's penis is inserted into four deep slits alongside the shaft of a man's penis!

A rather more sophisticated form of enlargement which entails drawing out the root of the penis that is hidden inside the body was pioneered in 1984 by a modern Chinese surgeon, Dr Long Dau-Chou. Although his work has attracted interest in the West – especially in America – it doesn't excite everyone, including the Beverly Hills urologist Dr D.S. Danoff, who commented a few years ago: 'You can't make an erect penis longer than it is. You can only create the illusion of length through these techniques. If you want a larger penis, you can save yourself $4,000 by putting it on a wooden block and slamming it with a hammer.'

IT'S THE STUFFING THAT COUNTS

Because of the undoubted demand for penis enlargement, the practice has become something of a speciality of unregistered 'surgeons' in the Far East, according to a report in the *Bangkok Post* of 12 October 1993. The story requires no comment:

Charlatan physicians have performed at least 100 bogus penis-enlargement operations in Thailand this year. The operations have involved injections of a mixture of olive oil, chalk and various other substances.

A Chaing Mai hospital spokesman commenting on the alarming rise in the number of these operations said, 'Male patients have come to us for attention in the most unhappy condition. We have even seen men with penises containing portions of the Bangkok Telephone Directory . . .

VAGINA DENTATA

One of the most bizarre sexual motifs, the toothed vagina, is to be found in Indian mythology throughout North and South America, and was for many generations claimed to actually occur in certain women. According to the tradition of the Chaco Indians, the first men in the world were unable to have sexual intercourse with their wives and it required all the energy of the cultural hero, Chaco, to break the teeth of the women's vaginas. Another tribe, the Waspishiana Indians, believed the first woman had a carnivorous fish inside her vagina. In an Indian hero tale from the USA – *Sun Tests his Son-in-Law* – the creation of sexual pleasure is attributed to one such woman:

> There was once a man who encountered a woman who invited him to have intercourse with her. She had had many men, but they had all died because of her toothed vagina. The hero was cleverer than all of them, however, and first inserted sticks in her vagina. The first of these she ground up, but the teeth were unable to chew up the harder ones. At this, the man knocked out all the remaining teeth, except leaving one [the clitoris] to allow her pleasure . . .

Rembrandt f. 634.

THE SERPENT WITHIN . . .

In Europe, as early as the Renaissance period, young men of good breeding were warned about sexually voracious women in language that mixed intimidation with health warnings. These are typical couplets that dated from the Middle Ages and were still being repeated during the Elizabethan era in England and across Europe:

> He that doth pursue virgins be warned that serpents lie waiting within their bodies to wound the penis . . .

> Those that are immoderate in conjoining with loose women do risk many maladies including blindness and the gout . . .

> Remember that fifteen hens will satisfy one cock, but fifteen men are not enough for one women . . .

> He that would woo a widow must go stiff before . . .

A SECRET, PRIVY PLACE

Aside from being one of the world's great satirists, François Rabelais (1494–1553) also studied medicine and was for a time a physician at Lyon. Some of his experiences at the hospital in the town may well have helped inform his unique books of wit, wisdom and the type of ribaldry to which he has subsequently given his name. In *Gargantua* (1534) he provides a typically bawdy description of women's genitals as they were then regarded by the medical community. It comes in a scene where Panurge consults Doctor Rondibilis about whether or not he should get married. Rondibilis tells him chauvinistically that Nature seems to have thought more of giving men 'a pleasant companion rather than producing a thing perfect and praiseworthy in itself' and continues waggishly:

Nature hath posited in a privy, secret place of their bodies, a sort of member (by some not impertinently termed an animal) which is not to be found in men. Therein sometimes are engendered certain humours so saltish, brackish, clammy, sharp, nipping, tearing, prickling and most eagerly tickling, that by their stinging acrimony, rending nitrosity, figging itch, wriggling mordancity and smarting salsitude (for the said member is of a most quick and lively feeling), their whole body is shaken and ebrangled, their senses totally ravished and transported, the operations of their judgement and understanding utterly confounded, and all disordinate passions and perturbations of the mind thoroughly and absolutely allowed, admitted and approved of, because this terrible animal is knit into, and hath union with, all the chief and most principal parts of the body . . .

Apparently inspired by this, an anonymous English author shortly thereafter published a volume entitled *Fanny Thoughtless*.

ERECTION IN WOMEN

Nicholas Culpeper (1616–54) is, of course, famous for his guide to herbs, *Culpeper's Herbal*, first published in 1653 and still in print today. He was also an astrologer and physician with a special interest in human sexuality and from this came his *Physical Directory* (1654). The book was controversial for several reasons – firstly, for his use of the term 'yard' to describe the penis (apparently so called because 'it hangs from the belly') which thereafter became the commonplace term for almost two hundred years; and, secondly, because he seems to have understood the role of the clitoris years ahead of his time. He wrote: 'The action of the clitoris in women is like that of the yard in men, which is erection, and its outer end is like the glans in men is in the greatest copulation, so is this in women.'

TAKING THE POLLEN TEST

Until our permissive age, men have always placed a high price on virginity and made great demands on premarital chastity. Suspicion – and plain distrust – have haunted the lives of countless men and women over the centuries and consequently produced a whole series of measures to 'guard and preserve virginity'. One of the most famous of these has undoubtedly been the chastity belt (of which more later), but there have been other 'Trials and Tests of Chastity' which, it was claimed, would reassure a husband that his bride was the perfect package of goods. One of the earliest books on this subject was published in 1615 bearing the name of the great philosopher Albertus Magnus – although, like Aristotle before him, he had nothing to do with its creation – entitled *Alberti Magni de Secretis Mulierum* (About the Secrets of Women). Written in Latin, it offered this simple, yet apparently foolproof, method for any suspicious bridegroom to discover the truth about his lady: 'Collect together some pollen of yellow lilies and give them to her to swallow. If she be pure, then nought will happen. But if she has lost her virginity, then she will be unable to contain the motion of her bladder and will urinate copiously.'

THE VIRGIN STING

A century later, another book on the same topic enjoyed equal success. Again the author was anonymous – one 'Albertus Parvus' – and his work, *Libellus de Mirabilibus Naturae Aracanis* (A Book on the Miraculous Panacea of Nature, 1729), unashamedly lifted many of Albertus Magnus's ideas. Parvus repeated the pollen method – suggesting *coaldust* in its place, or alternatively, yellow amber, china dust or burweed leaves if the unhappy bride gagged at such an ingredient! – and he declared that in some countries a freshly picked lettuce thrust under the woman's nose would produce the same result. Parvus's *pièce de resistance*, though, was the 'Bee-Test':

> It is a well known fact that even the most irritable bees become gentle when they are approached by a pure virgin and will not sting her. But should she go near a hive immediately after the loss of her innocence, then she will be attacked at once and her secret revealed for all to see. The reason for this remarkable proof is that bees are of but one sex and they abhor all lewdness and libertinism . . .

Le Remède

THE PILLOW CASE . . .

Other bizarre virginity tests flourished throughout the eighteenth and nineteenth century. When the 'one sex' nature of bees was disproved, this theory was replaced with another that claimed they could somehow 'sense' when a woman had been penetrated by a man, and it was his masculine exhalation which infuriated them. In a curious book, the *Medizinische Anekdoten*, published in Leipzig in 1767, it was stated that many men of the church had the ability to tell by the smell of a woman whether she was chaste or not, and cited dozens of examples including a blind friar in Vienna who could apparently tell a non-virgin from thirty paces! (Rather earlier than this, in 1251, the aptly named Bishop Robert Grosseteste, the Bishop of Lincoln, claimed to be able to tell whether nuns had kept their vows by squeezing their breasts to see if any milk could be extracted!) More extraordinary still was the 'infallible' and apparently long-lived method to test *any* woman's chastity by using a precious stone. It is described in the *Magiae Naturalis Libri* (1589) by Giambattista della Porta (1543–1615), the Italian who wrote on physiognomy, natural magic and gardening as well as penning several comedies:

Place a magnetised stone under the wife's pillow. Its miraculous effect will soon become evident. If the lady is faithful, she will nestle against her husband in her sleep and embrace him fervently. The unfaithful woman will simply roll off the bed as if an invisible hand had pushed her off . . .

THE SHEER NECK!

A German physician of the early nineteenth century, C.G. Flitner, made a special study of chastity tests and recorded a number of curious examples. One, which he said dated back to Roman times, involved measuring a woman's *neck*. Apparently a piece of thread had to be used to measure the distance from the tip of a maiden's nose to the point on the top of the head where the sagittal and lambdoid sutures meet. If the thread of this length reached around her neck, she was still chaste; if not, she had lost her virginity. Dr Flitner also discovered a variation on the pillow test, equally ancient. In this instance, the tongue of a wild duck and a toad had to be laid over the heart of a woman while she was asleep. She could then be questioned about her chastity, would answer truthfully, and awake unaware that she had been sleep-talking. The result of all the doctor's research – and, it must be added, a lengthy study of women in contemporary German society – enabled him to publish in Berlin in 1825 a 'tell-tale' list of *The Indications of Chastity in Women*:

Body-part Examined	Virgin	Non-Virgin
Eyes	Bright & Clear	Sad & Lowered
White of Eye	Pure	Clouded
Face	White & Smooth	Spotty
Nose	Fleshy	Thin
Neck	Slim & Thin	Thick
Voice	Pleasant & Melodious	Hoarse
Appetite	Good	Poor
Bosom	Good & Medium-sized	Large & Flabby

GRAND REVIEW OF THE WINDSOR CAMP.

THE VENUS VESTALS

A secret girls-only society founded in France in the seventeenth century claimed to have established the twenty-seven virtues that enabled a woman to be potentially the perfect sexual partner. Although just how these virtues had been arrived at was never made clear, a number of monks and nuns were believed to be among the 'selection council'. It was also said that any 'Venus Vestal' had to possess a minimum of sixteen virtues *and* be able to demonstrate them to the others to gain entry. The full list of feminine charms reads:

> A perfect complexion, blonde hair, snow-white teeth, lily-white skin, eyebrows darker than the darkest eyes, rose-pink nails, lips and cheeks, long hands and long hair, small teeth, ears and feet, a high forehead, an ample breast, the hips of a vase, two hand-spans of waist, a tiny mouth, a small nose and head, fine hair, delicate lips, dainty fingers, and lip-resistant nipples, a curved belly and succulent private parts . . .

There was also a catch for each beauty. *She must never have had sex with a man . . .*

A TASTE LIKE BIRDS' EGGS

The nature of the female ovum was not actually understood until the
end of the nineteenth century, which gave rise to all sorts of medical
nonsense such as this paragraph from an anonymous eighteenth-
century pamphlet, *Secrets of Nature in the Production of Man*:

> Our modern authors [sic] affirm that the ancients were very
> erroneous: for the testicles in women are but two eggs, like
> those of fowls. Neither have they any such office as those of
> men, but are indeed an ovarium, a receptacle for eggs, wherein
> they are nourished by the sanguinary vessels dispersed through
> them. The truth of this, they say, is so plain that if you boil
> them, they will have the same taste, colour and consistency
> with the taste of birds' eggs . . .

But boiled for three minutes or four?

THE SIXTH SENSE OF SEX

A nineteenth-century French physician, Paul Moreau, claimed in
his worthy but offbeat book *Des Aberrations du Sens Genetique*,
published in 1887, that women possessed not only the normal five
senses – seeing, hearing, smelling, tasting and feeling – but had a
sixth sense, too: the 'Genital Sense'. He explained: 'The Genital
Sense, which is inborn to women like the other five, can also be
injured psychically and physically. Usually such injury results
from a hereditary taint, leaving a predisposition to perversion, and
it is a phenomenon that requires the most intimate study.'
  Something fishy about this . . .?

THE OVARY OF A HIPPOPOTAMUS

In 1932, a biologist in the Soviet Union, Dr Anton Nemilov,
published *The Biological Tragedy of Women*, in which he claimed

that women's sex organs had 'developed phylogenetically ahead of man'. Hormones had discriminated unfairly between the male and female, he insisted, 'though the capitalistic and bourgeois societies will pay no attention to what they will regard as nonsense'. Nemilov believed it was time for women to be accepted as comrades and fully fledged members of the new proletariat state, and concluded in the typically leaden but unconsciously humorous Russian style of the time:

> We will not enter into details which are not important to our basic theme. We merely desire to point out that the most essential part of women's sexual apparatus, the ovary, or woman's sex gland, constitutes one five-thousandth part of the weight of her entire body, whereas in a cow the proportion is one fifty-thousandth part. Consequently woman's ovaries are proportionately heavier than those of ruminants. Dentici, who in 1922 analysed the sex organs of the hippopotamus, found that the ovary of this enormous animal differs only slightly in size from the ovary of woman.

THE CHASTITY OF WOMEN ACT

Although popular legend has it that there was once a 'Chastity of Women Act' on the English statute books in the prudish Victorian era intended to protect women against any insinuations on their honour, the truth is actually much stranger. The historian E.S. Turner has explained all in his amusing collection *An ABC of Nostalgia*, published in 1984:

> The 'Chastity of Women Act' actually refers to the 'Slander of Women Act', a curious and almost unheard-of measure which was introduced in 1891 to rectify what Lord Macnaghten called 'a very cruel state of the law'. It laid down that anyone falsely calling a woman a whore, a slut, a trollop, a soiled dove, a demirep or anything else in that class was liable in damages. The Marquess of Salisbury wished it to be made clear that 'only

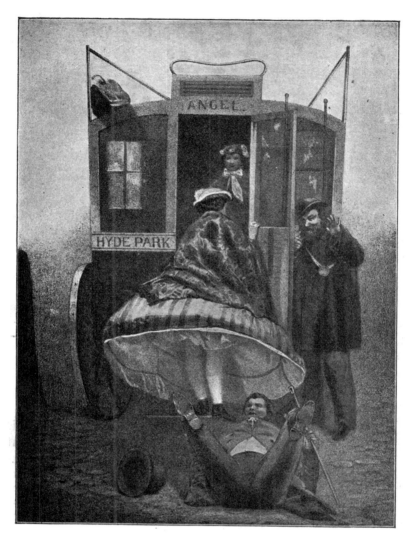

modest women would be eligible to sue'. Lord Selbourne forecast that the courts would be 'flooded with frivolous actions arising from tittle-tattle'. No such flood occurred, nor so far as one can discover, was there even a trickle. There was also never a 'Slander of Men Act' to protect them from being called rakes and goats!

THE LURE OF PERFUME

The use of perfume on and around the sex organs has been documented from Roman times to the present day. There have, though, been few stranger blends than the 'Magic Lure Perfume' which was marketed for over a century in America. No details of its composition were ever given – though the instructions for its use were very explicit:

> WOMEN should apply about 1 drop on each jaw [sic] of the vagina. This will make you more sexually exciting to men . . .

> MEN should apply about 2 drops to the male organ. This will enlarge the organ and attract women of your sexual desire.

RIDING ON HIGH

The application of ointment to the erogenous zones has now been established as the reason why witches once believed they could fly. A liberal application to the vagina, pudenda and breasts of a mixture of atropine and belladonna induced highly suggestive visions in the minds of these women, who then imagined themselves having sex with the Devil. In his book *Devils, Drugs and Doctors* (1929), W.H. Haggard explains:

> It thus happened that respectable matrons admitted to their father confessors that after rubbing the ointment on their bodies they felt as though they had involuntarily ridden by night over fields and meadows, and that when their steed leaped over any water it was like someone having intercourse with them in a most voluptuous way. We have, therefore, a direct admission of the connection between the witch-ride and union with Satan.

DOCTORS RECOMMEND REAST'S PATENT

INVIGORATOR CORSETS.

FOR LADIES, MAIDS, BOYS, GIRLS, AND CHILDREN.

Dr. M. O. B. NEVILLE, L.R.C.P., Edin. Medical Officer of Health, says, Nov. 1st, 1890 :—
" From a scientific point or view, I am of opinion that your Corset is the only one that gives support without unduly compressing important organs. Its elasticity, in a great measure, prevents this. I am satisfied, by its support of back and shoulders, that it is a material help to expanding the chest."

" Mrs. WELDON'S FASHION JOURNAL," says July '90 :—
" Undoubtedly supplies a long-felt want for ensuring an upright form and graceful carriage, COMBINES ELEGANCE of FORM WITH COMFORT. It renders a corset what it should be, comfort, and support to the wearer, strengthening the spine, expanding the chest, and giving necessary support without tight lacing or undue pressure."

PRICES.
Child's under 5 years, 3/4 ; Boys' and Girls' over 5 years, 4/6 ; Maids, 5/6 ; Ladies', 6/6, 8/6, 12/9, 18/6, 22/6, 63/-.

SOLD BY ALL DRAPERS, OR SENT P.O. TO
REAST, 15, CLAREMONT, HASTINGS, ENGLAND.
FOR LICENSE FOR MANUFACTURING, OR SALE OF AMERICAN PATENT APPLY AS ABOVE.
[1893]

THE UNMENTIONABLE PARTS

The Victorians took prudery to fantastic extremes because of their fears of sex, excretion and the body, according to G. Rattray Taylor in his book *Sex in History* (1953). Women, he says, were *ex definitione* sexless, hardly existed below the waist, or if they did, certainly did *not* have legs. He cites some wonderfully comic examples of this phenomenon:

> When advertisements for underclothing first began to appear in Victorian papers, the bifurcated [divided] garments were always shown folded so that the bifurcation would not be remarked upon. Any medical complaint between the neck and the knees was referred to as the 'liver', and when it was necessary to examine a female patient, she was more often than not handed a doll upon which the location of the affected part might be pointed out.
>
> So delicate did the sensibilities of the Victorians become, so easily were their thoughts turned to sexual matters, that the most innocent actions were taboo in case they might lead to lurid imaginings. It became indelicate to offer a lady a *leg* of chicken – hence the still surviving tradition that she is offered the breast; but even the breast could not be so called and became the 'bosom'. This – at least as applied to chickens – was an American refinement, as was the fitting of piano legs with crinolines! Though not, it seems, chair legs, which were presumably too thin to inspire lascivious thoughts . . .

And as for the *chaise longue* . . . unspeakable!

BEWARE GAUZE UNDERWEAR

An American physician with the delightful name of Dr Emma Angel Drake of Boston, warned of dire times ahead for girls who were not careful about what they wore during their periods. Writing in *What a Woman of Forty-Five Ought to Know* (1902), Dr

Drake browbeat her readers:

> Women who, as young girls, have been negligent of care at the menstrual period, who have danced, or exercised excessively in other ways without regard to this time, though they may or may not, as a consequence, have suffered at the periods thereafter, yet at the menopause they will be quite likely to pay the debt of abused nature, by sufferings which bear at least some proportion to their negligence. Girls have been allowed to make very great change in their dress in winter time, *even removing flannels for low necked gauze underwear*, in order that they might dress according to the prevailing style for evening parties, and what wonder that invalidism, when so coveted, is found? Though through the vigor of their constitution, they may seem to bear up for many years, yet physical vigor is sapped, and at the crisis, when a reserve force is needed, they find themselves without it, and go down with the current to days of suffering, if not to death itself . . .

It's flannels or a fate that *is* death, girls!

BREECHED FOR FAILURE

In an attack on colleges that allowed girls to dress and behave in an unseemly fashion – wearing knee breeches and using words such as 'devilish' and 'damned' – the New York educator Ralph Wait Parsons warned that such liberties could affect their future love life. In the *New York Medical Journal* in 1907, Parsons wrote:

> Such women as these will never be able to fulfill their female functions, for not only will their reproductive apparatus be stunted by education, but no man will ever love them because men only have deep sentiment for women with the feminine traits of character with which God intended they should be endowed.

The only way to put things right, according to Parsons, was that girls should not learn Latin, Greek, Higher Maths or political economy, 'but spend most of their time in home economic classes'.

OVARY POWER

There were also words of warning about excesses of femininity in 1916 from the English gynaecologist William Blair Bell. In his book *The Sex Complex*, he stated that the gonads did not act alone to influence female characteristics and genital functions, going on:

> Sexual and maternal capacity depends upon the proportion of femininity in each individual woman's make-up. It is my contention that ovarian insufficiency in women is capable of treatment by what is known as Organotherapy. However, excessive ovarian secretion which manifests itself in women who are extremely feminine in appearance and character will produce excessive sexuality, amounting perhaps to sexual insanity, leading to masturbation or even inversion.

THE FORNICATORS

Albert Ellis, the American writer who became famous for his books on sexual attitudes during the forties and fifties, devoted a chapter in his book *The Folklore of Sex* (1951) to 'Fornication'. His comments are both salutary and amusing:

> On an unconscious level, we may be sure, contemporary conflicts over pro- and anti-fornicative are confused indeed. Legion is the number of those men who madly jump into the arms of the first girl who will have them – only to find themselves physically impotent. Or who resist all temptations to go out with girls – only to find themselves compulsively exhibiting their genitals before teenage girls . . .
>
> And multitudinous are those girls who break off their

engagements because their fiancés insist on their having premarital sex relations, only to wind up with psychosomatically caused allergies, high blood pressure, or other symptoms. Or who gaily copulate with half-a-dozen boys before their marriage – only to acquire an acute case of dyspareunia (painful intercourse) on their wedding night . . .

THE BAMBOOZLERS OF WOMEN

Back in the thirties – long before the current campaign about the dangers of smoking – cigarettes were accused by a vociferous group in America as being a direct threat to the female sex drive. In leaflets circulated throughout many states, cigarettes were declared to be the 'Bamboozlers of Women' which could rob them of everything from feminine charm to beauty. It added: 'Cigarette smoking is becoming the outstanding sex sin of the United States. The sensation of sucking a cigarette gives abnormal stimulus to the sex instincts and often leads to moral turpitude . . .'

A PROMISCUOUS WORLD

In a series of articles in the *Journal of Venereal Disease Information* in 1949, a group of clinical psychologists agreed that all promiscuous girls were 'wayward and lacked self-respect' and would always 'fail to give their sexual partners satisfaction'. One of the psychologists, Dr John F. Stokes, also confessed that he had a nightmare vision about what might happen if a cure for syphilis and gonorrhea – a natural result of all this promiscuity – was actually *discovered*: 'The elimination of venereal disease would bring mankind to its fall instead of its fulfilment and lead to a world of accepted, universalised and safeguarded promiscuity.'

THE FEAR OF TAMPONS

In 1950, the *American Journal of Psychotherapy* published the results of an extensive survey into the fallacies concerning menstruation. The magazine listed a number of nonsensical notions still held by many young girls throughout the country – passed on by mothers, grandmothers or other female friends – which medical advice had been quite unable to overturn. These included:

* Never have a permanent wave put in your hair during a period.
* Never get your teeth filled at the time of menstruation.
* The only thing to relieve period pains are hot drinks.

The authors of the survey, Thomas Abel and Natalie Joffe, also said that many young females believed tampons were actually dangerous: 'There are millions of our girls who refuse to use tampons because they feel that by using them their virginity is in some way tampered with . . .'

3.

THE ART OF BED WRESTLING

Almost as long as men and women have been having sex, there have been arguments about the best position to do it. Fragmentary records from the Babylonian era show that face to face, with the woman on her back, was the usual position – although there were evidently variations on the theme, including anal entry, oral sex and homosexuality.

Over the years, of course, the bed has become accepted as most people's idea of the best place for love-making; though here again the argument between the 'missionary position' and all the rest has never gone away. An American physician who one hopes felt up to his name, Dr Fitzgeorge Feelgood, is just one among many who have championed the tried and tested. He wrote in a pamphlet, *The Supreme Contact*, published in 1961:

> A doctor, who is a professor in a very large university, has recommended that the bodies of husband and wife in coition ought to be across each other, forming a cross, instead of face to face. If God be our authority, and the Bible our approach, it refutes and voids all such nonsense immediately. It is not through ignorance, but on authority, that I say dogmatically, marital coitus should be in the general position of the love embrace – face to face – since God ordained this act for humans to be that occasional supreme expression of love.

Not everyone agrees, of course. The following advertisement appeared in a Los Angeles newspaper only a short while ago:

> Through the centuries, men have experimented with different sexual positions. For a detailed diagram and written explanation of the *'Possible Original Method of Sex'* send $10 for Method 6891 . . .'

What on earth are the other 6,890!

THE ART OF BED WRESTLING

Titus Flavius Domitianus, who became Roman emperor in AD 81, was a man who made war as ferociously as he made love. Sometimes even more so – and it was his cruelties to all and sundry that led to a conspiracy against him and his eventual assassination in AD 96. He is, though, remembered for a memorable epithet: 'Copulation is a form of physical exercise to which a man must devote himself with all his courage and strength. I have named it "Bed Wrestling".'

There is, sadly, no record as to whether Domitianus required more than two throws for a submission.

A LITTLE OF A BAD THING

The Roman physician Aulus Cornelius Celsus, who lived during the first century AD, was also a man of war – as well as a philosopher, agriculturist and master of rhetoric. However, as he revealed in his book *De Medicina*, he did not share Domitianus's taste in physical jerks. 'Sexual intercourse neither should be avidly desired, nor should it be feared very much. Rarely performed, it revives the body. Performed frequently, it weakens.'

Curiously, Celsus died in bed – having just had sex.

A CUT TOO DEEP?

Ibn Sina Avicenna (980–1037) was an Arab philosopher and physician who busied himself in Persia looking after a number of lecherous sultans and their harems – which may well have given him his particular interest in sex. In any event, he calculated the cost of intercourse to a man, thus: 'It is my estimation that forty ounces of blood distil into one ounce of semen. Therefore it is as

Dedicated to the Choice Spirits of the High Burlesque.

weakening to lose one ounce of semen to a woman as to lose forty ounces of blood by cutting a vein.'

Pity there were no blood transfusions!

BLOOD AND FRICTIONS

Soranus (AD 93–138), an unfortunately named Greek physician, did not agree with most of his contemporaries that a man's semen was drawn from all parts of the body during coition. He wrote gushingly: 'As to the vehemence of pleasure in sexual intercourse, it is not because the semen comes from all the body, but because there is a strong friction. The pleasure is at the end act. Else it would be in different parts and not at the same time, coming [sic] sooner in some and later in others.'

Soranus was also an advocate of 'permanent virginity' because he believed that those who kept themselves *intacto* were 'less susceptible to disease'.

THE MADNESS OF WOMEN

'Any sexual excitement in women is a melancholic affliction,' declared the French psychiatrist Jean-Etienne Esquiril (1772–1840) in his *Des Maladies Mentales* (1838). The reason for this lay in the blood, he said, and there was only one answer. Reach for the whip. Esquiril explained: 'Females known to be suffering from sexual excitement are to be confined by their doctors in a *Carnificina* (medical torture house) and have their blood let. This bloodletting to be repeated 30 times in six days. It draws from the women, along with their blood, and at the same time, their insane minds and desire for mad love.'

And they called it a curse?

THE REMEDY OF VENUS

German physicians around this same time had a rather more pleasant cure for 'hysterical women' – what they called 'The Remedy of Venus'. In a word, sex. An anonymous pamphlet published in 1803 declared enthusiastically: 'The most powerful and most pleasant bodily sensations are derived from sleeping with a person of the opposite sex. Chiarugi maintains that it is also an excellent cure for melancholia.'

No doubt about it!

THE SEX CALENDAR

During the Middle Ages, the Christian Church actually decreed on which days married couples were permitted to have sex. Initially, it was made illegal on Sundays, Wednesdays and Fridays – which those who were good at mathematics quickly realised made sex off-limits for the equivalent of *five months in the year*. To compound matters, the Church authorities banned intercourse for forty days before Easter and Christmas as well as for three days before taking communion – and the regulations about attending communion were very strict. Just to make life really frustrating, sex was also forbidden from the time of conception to forty days after a birth. Historian George May commented wryly on this in *Social Control of Sexual Expression* (1930): 'The Church's attitude was thus strongly in contrast with that of the Mohammedans, who held that there were grounds for divorce if the sexual act was not performed at least once a week.'

It's what gets religion a bad name.

Before . . .

. . . and after

THE PICTURESQUE POSTURES

The Italian poet Pietro Aretino (1492–1557), who was famous for his wit, impudence and talents, won and then lost papal patronage as a result of his sixteen shameless *Sonetti Lussuriosi*. However, his charismatic personality and bawdy comedies found favour with a number of powerful Italian noblemen who acted as his sponsors and thereafter he enjoyed a productive and stylish life. He died, bizarrely, while laughing heartily at an outrageous adventure of one of his sisters, fell off a stool, and was killed on the spot. Aretino's own amatory adventures, in particular his delight in experimenting with different sexual positions, inspired such memorable lines as 'Place your leg, dearest, on my shoulder, and take my truncheon in your tender grasp,' and the following list of thirty-four 'Picturesque Postures':

* Pile on the Load
* Mount your Donkey

* Put the Box on the Barrel
* Greyhound Fashion
* Somersault Fashion (Press the Back)
* Show the Shepherd's Sundial
* Franc-Mason Fashion
* The Real Barbary Enema
* Contemplate the Beatitudes
* As done with the Crane's Foot
* The Jesuit Confession
* The Squeeze-Behind
* The Holy Ecstasy
* House your Guest
* The Seated Bag-Pipe
* The Christmas Candle

* The Good Spankass
* Taking as an Idea
* Making Sooty Candles
* Helping Old People
* Turning on a Pivot
* Take it in a Cart
* German Fashion
* The Sleeping Child
* Put on the Shoe
* Run after the Ring
* Ordinary or Good Christian Style
* The Frog
* Slanting Sex
* Cross-section Sex

* Splashing the Stream
* Moorish Fashion
* The Good Enema
* Stick the Two

CONJUGAL LEWDNESS

Daniel Defoe (1660–1731), the butcher's son whose career included stints as a merchant adventurer, government spy and outspoken pamphleteer (which earned him a term of imprisonment) was a man of robust opinions and strong sexuality. His 'Scandal Club' column in *The Review* tackled various contemporary sexual mores, while his novel *Moll Flanders* (1722) is one of the best of all tales of low life. Defoe also wrote dozens of political squibs, a fair amount of ribald poetry and a number of anonymous leaflets such as *Conjugal Lewdness* (1727), one of the earliest satires on sex manuals. In this he writes with his tongue probably very firmly in his cheek: 'It is sinful for married couples to copulate with the carnal enjoyment that men derive from whores.'

AN ANSWER TO 'SMELFUNGUS'

Another eighteenth-century writer of picaresque novels, Scots-born Tobias Smollett (1721–71), who was nicknamed 'Smelfungus' by one of his critics, first practised as a surgeon in London before making his name as the author of *Roderick Random* (1748) and *Peregrine Pickle* (1751), in both of which the heroes have amatory adventures. An enthusiastic traveller and ladies' man, Smollett delighted in satirising the morals of English society and it was this which earned him his popular epithet. In a memorable line in *Roderick Random*, for example, one of the characters, Strutwell, declares: 'Homosexuality gains ground apace and in all probability will become in a short time a more fashionable device than fornication.' Not everyone saw the humour in this, as Alex Comfort has explained in *The Anxiety Makers* (1967):

> The Commonwealth Act of 1650 had made fornication punishable by death, but the reactions were many and varied . . . In London, Smollett's *Roderick Random* with its references to fornication and homosexuality raised eyebrows in the same way as an extraordinary little pamphlet, the title of which speaks for itself: *An Essay Upon Improving and Adding to the Strength of Great Britain and Ireland by Fornication*. It was said to have been written by 'a Young Clergyman' – from Ireland, naturally!

THE PRICE OF CREATIVITY

The French author Honoré de Balzac (1799–1850), famous for the vibrant and sprawling series of books known as the *Comédie Humaine*, and the shorter, unashamedly bawdy *Contes Drôlatiques* (1833), was a writer of huge productivity. He often worked for between fifteen and eighteen hours a day and was fastidious in everything he wrote. Curiously, for someone who wrote so well about sex, the act itself he considered 'a drain on my creativity'. In fact, Balzac did not marry until late in life, and in the intervening years occasionally visited Parisian prostitutes. On one occasion,

A N

E S S A Y

UPON

IMPROVING and ADDING,

TO THE

STRENGTH

OF

GREAT-BRITAIN and *IRELAND,*

BY

FORNICATION,

JUSTIFYING

The fame from SCRIPTURE and REASON.

By a Young CLERGYMAN.

Omne tulit punctum qui mifcuit utile dulci.   Hor.

Gen. Chap. i. v. 28. *And God bleffed them, and faid unto them, Be fruitful, and multiply, and replenifh the Earth.* Chap. ix. v. 1. *And God Bleffed Noah and his Sons, and faid unto them, Be fruitful, and multiply, and replenifh the Earth.* v. 7. *And you, be ye fruitful, and multiply, bring forth abundantly in the Earth, and multiply therein.*

LONDON:

Printed in the Year M.DCC.XXXV.

after several months of abstinence, he gave way to his natural urges. But after leaving the brothel, he was heard to moan to a friend: 'I have just lost a novel this morning!'

VARIATIONS ON A THEME

In an essay on the female's desire for the unfamiliar in love-making, the French author Jean Jerome Romanet quotes some well-established, if unusual, examples of 'bed wrestling', in his book *Women A-Z* (1961). He writes:

> Orientals lay their ladies out on their tummies, and sprinkle their backs with millet grains, to encourage doves to come and peck. Alternatively, the Chinese pour milk into the navel for dwarf pigs to lap up.
>
> The Italians practise a variation on a French theme, what they call in cooking parlance the *pompido telecommando*, i.e. taking the beloved's thumb between their lips. The Germans, on the other hand, manufacture ingenious accessories on an industrial scale . . .

One pint or two?

THE PRICKLY SOLUTION

In the sixteenth century, many women in the more isolated rural districts of England were afraid that too much sex would turn them into witches. Historian Margaret Murray, in her study *The Witch Cult in Western Europe* (1921), tells us the lengths they resorted to: 'Rather than risk such a fate, the women turned to the root [sic] of the problem and tied pieces of holly to the end of the bed as this was supposed to make their menfolk less amorous.'

BUNDLING UP WELL

During the years of British rule in America, a curious bedroom activity developed known as 'bundling'. As tantalising as it must have been comic, the practice is explained here by historian Norman Gelb in his aptly titled book *The Irresistible Impulse* (1979):

> The practice of 'bundling' in which a young man and woman, usually fully dressed and usually in the presence of others (albeit in a darkened room), engaged in bed in usually low-keyed love play, had actually been successfully transmitted from Britain, Holland and Scandinavia by early settlers. In some parts of the colonies, it was called 'tarrying'. It existed in a setting where homes were small, usually consisting of only one room, fuel was in short supply both for lighting and heating, and where long work hours limited the opportunities for couples to court, particularly in winter.
>
> 'Bundling' also sometimes referred to the tradition of hospitality in remote regions where a passing stranger was permitted to share a bed for one night in an isolated farmhouse. Sometimes it was the bed of the young woman of the house which he shared – from which practice the bawdy 'travelling salesman' stories evolved . . .

THE SAFE DEFINITION

For all their reserve, the Victorians were also not above debating how often men and women – *married*, of course! – should have sex. One of the most forthright statements is to be found in *The Marriage Ideal* by the indefatigable chronicler of prostitution, William Acton, published in 1850. He writes:

> According to my experience, few hard-working, intellectual married men should indulge in connection oftener than *once* in seven or perhaps ten days. This, however, is only a guide for strong, healthy men. Generally, I should say that an individual may consider he has committed an *excess* coitus if succeeded by languor, depression of spirits, and malaise. This is the safest definition!

If the cap fits . . .

THE RUSSIAN POSITION

The Russians have given a lot of thought to the subject, too – with resulting opinions poles apart.

Catherine the Great was apparently a very highly sexed lady. She declared that *six times a day* was the ideal. This was particularly good for insomnia, she said.

In contrast, a Soviet scientist, Vladimir Belkin, wrote in a Russian medical journal that for sex to have the maximum effect for both partners, a study he had carried out suggested the optimum was . . . *two minutes*.

What took so long?

NEVER ON A FULL STOMACH

'Bed wrestling' after the kind of gargantuan meals that our ancestors used to eat was a definite no-no. Advice to this effect can be found in a number of documents, especially in the pages of the *Compendyous Regyment; or, a Dyetry of Health* by one Dr Andrew Borde, written in 1542. Dire consequences awaited those who took no notice of his words: 'Beware of veneyrous acts before the first sleep of the day. Especially beware of such things after lunch or after a full stomach, for it doth ingender the cramp and the gout and other displeasures.'

Takes the weight off your feet, though!

'AMATIVE EXCITEMENT'

A London hydrotherapist, T.L. Nichols, was another vigorous opponent of over-indulgence, which he referred to as 'amative excitement'. In his *Esoteric Anthropology* (1873), he declared that 'a healthy woman' (married, naturally) was only receptive to sex for *a few days each month when she is full of ardour*. Unfortunately, Nichols gave his male readers no hint as to when this might be, but he did advise the ladies how to avoid stirring up 'amative excitement' in their menfolk by not stimulating 'the organs of generation by immodest dressing, dancing and allowing kissing and caressing of the bosom'. He added by way of warning:

In the corrupt state of modern life, many women are not only incapable of sexual enjoyment, but can be deeply injured in their nervous system by the efforts of their husbands to make them participate in, and so heighten, their enjoyments. I further caution men that after fifty, sexual pleasures are very exhausting and liable to produce paralysis or apoplexy.

What a d——, b—— nerve!

BANNED VOLUMES

The Victorian obsession with decorum has produced many observations on what was right and proper – take this example in the section on 'The Bedroom' from *A Book of Etiquette for Ladies* by Lady Sarah Gough, published in 1863: 'The perfect wife will see to it that the works of male and female authors be properly separated on her bookshelves. Their proximity, unless they happen to be married, should not be tolerated.'

THE SINNER'S GUIDE

New students arriving at the University of Ohio in 1901 found a booklet entitled *A Guide for Young Students of Both Sexes* awaiting each and every one of them in their rooms. Two definitions were printed in red for extra emphasis:

VENAL SIN: Thinking about sexually stimulating things without a sufficient reason.

NO SIN: Thinking about sexually stimulating things with a sufficient reason.

Just give me a reason!

CEREMONIAL SEX

In 1915, an Australian, W.J. Chidley, published a controversial little book, *The Answer; or, The World as Joy*, in which he claimed to have discovered the 'true' method of love-making. The publication attracted the interest of doctors, sexologists and writers all over the globe who, in the main, professed themselves completely baffled by Chidley's idea. The British writer Norman Douglas declared after a meeting with him, 'I would have given a good deal if Mr. Chidley had obliged me with an oracular demonstration of his "correct method" which I hold to be physiologically impossible or else, if practicable, a sight worth seeing.' Havelock Ellis, author of the groundbreaking volume *The Psychology of Sex* (1933), was equally puzzled by the theory. Chidley explained his credo in these words, giving very little away:

> All crime, madness and misery of the human race is due to a false method of coitus. I have discovered the correct technique and, when the time is right, I will reveal this to the world and restore happiness to mankind. I also believe that sex should be performed publicly, on suitable occasions, with pomp and without shame . . .

Sadly, before Chidley was able to reveal his great secret – or specify the 'suitable occasions' – the Australian police arrested him, declared him insane, and locked him up.

THE SCIENCE OF STRUGGLE

What might be called a case of history repeating itself occurred in 1961 when London University issued *Notes for the Use of Bachelors of Science*. Under the heading of 'The Sciences' was a not-altogether-serious sentence which harked right back to the days of Titus Flavius Domitianus: 'The most useful and least taught science seems to us undoubtedly to be *Parthenomachia* (from the

Greek *parthenos*: virgin, and *mache*: combat). A struggle in the presence of young girls.'

And to the victor – the spoils!

PURER THAN DRIVEN SUGAR

The bedroom door has, of course, always closed on the sexual activities of the heroes and heroines in the hugely popular romantic and historical novels produced in their hundreds by Barbara Cartland, the lady who is often referred to as 'The Queen of Romance'. She is also a writer on health and physical fitness and her own remarkable longevity bears witness to her carefully regimented lifestyle. She has pronounced on sexual matters on several occasions, the two following statements – on white sugar and virginity – having caused particular interest:

> White sugar is the curse of civilisation – it causes fatigue and sexual apathy between husband and wife. My recipe against sexual fatigue is to take honey in large quantities; two Gev-E-Tabs, 10 vitamin E pills, four wheatgerm oil tablets, four vitamin A pills, four bonemeal tablets, six liver-plus tablets, two dessert spoons of Bio-Strath Elixir, twice a day . . .

> I'll wager you that in ten years time it will be fashionable again to be a virgin . . .

This last statement was, however, made in *1976*.

4.

FERTILITY RITES – AND WRONGS

Delorme Pinx.   Me Lépicié Sculpsit.

Urine has for centuries been claimed in European folklore as one of the most popular tests of fertility in men and women. However, there is more to it than just taking a pee, as this paragraph from a delightfully entitled eighteenth-century pamphlet, *A Private Looking Glass for the Female Sex*, informs its readers: 'To learn whether a man or woman be fertile, sprinkle the urine of the woman on one leaf of lettuce and the man on another. The one whose urine dries away the first is the unfruitful one.'

No instructions are given on the method of sprinkling, however . . .

THE PEE TEST

When a female becomes pregnant, urine can once again be relied upon to reveal the sex of the unborn child. Or at least according to a book, *Of the Signs of Conception*, which was also published in the eighteenth century though it evidently drew on material of a much earlier date: 'To tell whether the child be a boy or girl, go out early in the morning and plant a seed of wheat and a seed of barley. Then do piss upon the seeds in equal measure and await which of them sprouts first. If it be the wheat, then the child will be male; if it be the barley, then a girl.'

A NOSE FOR SMELLS

The same book also repeats a method of detecting whether infertility in a woman has been caused by what we would now call a prolapsed uterus. This test is said to have been first instituted by the Egyptians where the details were found on an ancient papyrus roll: 'Do apply sweet things to her nose and stinking things to the womb. This will cause it to seek the pleasant and fly from the stinking.'

The mind – and stomach – boggles!

THE MANUFACTURE OF MAN

The Arab philosopher and physician Avicenna (980–1037), who made a special study of sex and fertility in his part of the world, offered this amusing precis in his book *Canon of Medicine*, to what was then the current belief about the process of generation: 'It is like the manufacture of cheese. The male sperm is the equivalent to the clotting agent in milk and the female sperm to that of the coagulum. Since the starting point of clotting is in the rennet, so the starting point of the clot 'man' is in the male semen.'

So what a lot of clots we all are!

PATRON SAINTS OF FERTILITY

The desire for fertility among men and women resulted in the creation of a number of curious 'phallic saints' attributed with extraordinary powers. Among their number were St Guerlichon of Bourg Dieu in France, whose name became a synonym for prostitutes; St Guignole, the first abbé of Landevenec, who got his reputation by mistaken association with the word *gignère*, from the French 'to beget'; and St René in Anjou through confusion with *reins*, kidneys, which for many years were actually believed to be the source of sexual power! All of these holy men were accredited with large genitals and their statues equipped with huge phalli. The most extraordinary of all, though, was St Foutin, of whom Payne Knight has written in *An Account of the Worship of Priapus* (1886):

> Foremost among these phallic saints was St. Foutin created by assimilation of the name of Pothin, the first Bishop of Lyons, to the verb *foutre*. When the Protestants took Embrun in 1585, they found men and women worshipping the phallus of St. Foutin and pouring wine on it, hence his sobriquet, 'le sainte vinaigre'. Women wishing to conceive would make use of the phallus in the same way that Roman wives would, before entering the marriage bed, make use of the wooden phallus of Mutunus Tutunus.

Such phallic practices continued long after the Middle Ages. In 1786, the British Minister in Naples wrote about a part of Isernia where the peasants worshipped 'the great toe of St. Cosmo' – i.e. his phallus. During a three-day feast peasants, chiefly women, would kiss waxen models and give them to the priest saying, 'Blessed St. Cosmo, that's how I want it to be'! Men would also present their members to the priest to be anointed with oil, and 1,400 flasks of oil were consumed every year for this purpose.

THE LOSS OF BINKUM BANKUM

In Britain in medieval times, when the widow of a land holder formed a sexual relationship with another man, her lands could be forfeited by law. However, in certain districts, a contrite widow could have this ruling overturned by performing a ceremony which would also apparently restore her sexuality, 'if she had become impotent by her immoral behaviour'. The ritual consisted of attending a court meeting *riding backwards on a black ram clutching its tail in her hand* and repeating the words:

Here I am, riding upon a black ram,
Just like the whore I am.
And for my crinkum crankum,
Have lost my binkum bankum.
And for my tail's game,
Have brought to this world shame.
Therefore good master steward,
Let me have my lands again.

A HANDY CURE

A particularly grisly remedy for infertile women was apparently
quite widespread in Britain and Europe from the late Middle Ages
onwards. It was customary for criminals to be hung on gallows in
many public places to serve as a warning to other wrong-doers.
But fear could not keep away females who hankered after children,
according to George Ryley Scott in his book *Curious Customs of
Sex and Marriage* (1933):

> The belief in the special powers of a dead body, especially those
> hung for criminal deeds, was there for everyone to see on the
> Gibbets. Those which were minus hands or feet had received
> the attention of desperate women who believed that by taking
> and keeping these limbs infertility would be cured. And it was
> not only the peasants who took such liberties with the dead,
> but high-born members of society, albeit that they probably
> sent their servants to perform the actual butchery . . .

A STINGING SOLUTION . . .

Marginally less unpleasant – though definitely more painful – was
the 'Nettle Cure' which had apparently been first devised by the
Romans as a cure against impotence. It is to be found recorded in
a voluminous work on syphilis written by the French physician
Girandeau de Saint-Gervais in 1841. In his book, the author also

describes the case of an impotent man who habitually rubbed musk on his penis until, one day, it swelled to such an extent that he 'remained coupled to his wife, joined like two dogs'. According to Saint-Gervais, the 'Nettle Cure' was only one of several cures in which pain being inflicted upon the genitals was said to cure impotence, but this, he believed, was the most successful: 'The genitals are to be rubbed with green nettle leaves, freshly picked. The rubbing must be vigorous so that the burning to the parts is hotter. In particularly difficult cases, the nettles should be woven into whips, and the genitals and public parts flogged heartily . . .'

THE SIGNS OF INFERTILITY

That famous seventeenth-century volume, *Aristotle's Masterpiece*, well thumbed by succeeding generations of readers, could, of course, be relied upon to provide some advice on fertility in men and women. The author addressed the sexes individually:

TO A MAN LOOKING FOR A WIFE:
It is advisable that a man look carefully at a prospective wife for signs of infertility. Remember that little women are more likely to conceive than gross women, slender more than fat, and a woman with swelling breasts much more so than a woman who is flat-chested.

TO A WOMAN LOOKING FOR A HUSBAND:
A man may be sterile because the ligaments of his yard are distorted or broken, thus preventing the passage of the seed or because of a defect in the testes. He may even be sterile through over-indulgence in food and drink.

'DOCTOR' SIBLY'S LUNAR TINCTURE

Ebenezer Sibly was an eighteenth-century quack responsible for the invention of two bizarre medicines, a 'Solar Tincture for Men' and 'Lunar Tincture for Women'. Apart from these cure-alls for sexual problems, he also wrote *The Medical Mirror; or Treatise on the Impregnation of the Human Female Shewing the Origin of Diseases and the Principles of Life and Death* which was first published in 1770. Sibly's particular concern was for young virgins – and the merchandising of his tinctures, as this extract from his book reveals:

In the eye of common observation, the sallow and inanimate virgin, by coition, often becomes plump and robust, beautiful and active; whilst the widow, or married woman deprived of commerce with her husband, gradually returns to the imperfections and peculiarities of single life; and the ancient virgin, all her life deprived of this animating effluvia, is generally consumed with infirmity, ill-temper, or disease. It is well-known that the want of coition at the time of life when nature seems to require it, lays the foundation of many disorders in females. In this manner, I am sorry to remark, are thousands of the most delicate and lovely women plunged into eternity . . .

But there is an answer to snatch the unhappy patient from the arms of death. The best method of regimen is laid down in my *Family Physician*, page 217, which, if well observed, in addition to the following course, will perform a cure. Take leaves of mugwort, briony, and penny-wort, of each a handful; infuse them four days in two quarts of soft water, and then pour off the clear liquor for use. Take a gill-glass, three-parts full, with forty drops of my *Lunar Tincture* added to it, three times a day – viz., morning, noon, and night – till the decoction be all used. For this malady, this is the only specific hitherto known; it unclogs the genital tubes, purges and cools the uterus and vagina, cleanses the urinary passages, dissolves viscid humours in the blood, sharpens the appetite, stimulates the nerves and invigorates the spirits!

How much a bottle, Doctor?

TAKING THE WATERS

There were equally curious medicines available for men at this time. One product much advertised was the 'True Cordial Quintessence of Vipers' for 'the real substantial Cure of Impotency in Men'. Also on sale was the 'Bath Restorative' aimed more particularly at those gentlemen whose sex life was beginning to flag. An advertisement from the *Morning Post* of 6 January 1776 sang the praises of this 'restorative balm warranted to revive any Constitution that is not absolutely mouldered away'. Among the claims made for it were:

* In the late decays of life it will supply the vital lamp with some recruits!
* It is admirable for those who have been almost worn out by women and wine!!

* Where persons are not early happy in their conjugal embraces, it will render their intercourse prolific!!!
* It will also be of service to our rising generation!!!!

WHY IRISH EYES ARE SMILING . . .

William Brodum, an eighteenth-century quack doctor who practised in London, believed in bathing the genitals in icy water as a stimulant and eating raw eggs as an aphrodisiac. Those who avoided meat made the most fertile lovers, he declared in his book *A Guide to Old Age; or, A Cure for the Indiscretions of Youth* (1795), and he favoured one group of females above all others: 'What is it that makes the Irish ladies such excellent bed companions? They run in the open air, and eat of good mealy potatoes broken down in milk . . .'

FALLING FOR FERTILITY

In 1938, infertile women in Yorkshire, England were offered a curious – if not actually dangerous – cure for their problem. The idea came from a part-time student of medicine who was also a keen amateur pilot. William Lyster claimed to have found a guaranteed way of ensuring conception as a result of his dual interests: he would take them flying in his aircraft and, when his passengers least expected it, plunge the machine into a loop-the-loop. He explained his theory with masterful brevity: 'The force of gravity as the aircraft turns over will thereupon open up the fallopian tubes.'

EXPOSED TO DANGER

According to a survey conducted as recently as 1951, there were still a number of rural areas in the mid-western American states where young girls believed in an old saw that any girl who exposed her breasts ('one or both', it was said) before she got married, was in danger of becoming infertile. The survey in, of all publications, the *Farm Quarterly*, reported that wearing a bathing suit was just as bad, especially if any of a female's 'private parts' could be seen 'or their presence was indicated'. Clearly some free spirits were prepared to take a risk, because the *Quarterly* also noted another equally firmly held viewpoint: 'Any boy who climbs a tree to spy on a girl getting undressed is fit to be burned alive.'

Enough to put any Peeping Tom or Dick off!

THE INVISIBLE PENIS

In the Middle Ages, impotence in men and women was often attributed to witchcraft. The use of charms and conjurations by witches was said to be the cause of any number of pathological sexual phenomena which 'hath hindered men from performing the sexual act and women from conceiving'. The *Malleus Maleficarum* described the bizarre story of a young man who had 'an intrigue with a girl and, upon leaving her, lost his member'. For days, the young man searched for the girl – who he was convinced must be a witch – in order to recover his missing penis. The story continues:

> Finally coming across the girl he seized her, wound a towel tightly around her neck, and threatened to choke her unless she restored his manhood. At this the witch touched him with her hand between the thighs and said, 'Now you have what you desire.' And the young man felt his member had been restored to him. But it must in no way be believed that such members are really torn right away from the body, but that they are hidden by the devil through some prestidigitatory art, so that they can be neither seen nor felt.

WHO STOLE MY PARTS?

Fear of witchcraft is still very prevalent in Africa, and in late 1990, panic swept through the male population of Lagos, the capital of Nigeria, when rumours began to spread that a number of sorcerers were stealing men's private parts: though for what reason was unclear. Apparently, these masters of witchcraft – who could turn themselves invisible at will – snatched the vital parts by merely touching their victims. A subsequent report of the events in the *Lagos Mail* stated that within a week of the first rumours, hysteria had spread to other cities in the country. It continued:

> A riot in Enugu was typical of the kind of incidents fear of penis-napping caused. A man boarding a bus shouted out that his family jewels had disappeared. The man in front of him was dragged off the bus and beaten. Fearing a lynching, a policeman fired warning shots, which only made matters worse. He accidentally killed the bus driver and injured a woman and her child.
>
> There are reports of at least four suspected sorcerers being beaten to death by frightened mobs, and a complete breakdown

of public order seemed imminent as hundreds were arrested for spreading harmful rumours. The Deputy Police Commissioner, James Danbana, made an announcement denying the stories. But then a second rumour also began to circulate – that women's breasts were being snatched . . .

A good spell, it seems, never lies down . . .

THE GREEK FOR FERTILITY

The Ancient Greeks made something of a science of devising ways to ensure fertility for their womenfolk. In a study of Greek medicines and remedies in *The Medical News* of July 1965, Dr Thomas Thurlow reported:

> The Greeks believed that fertility could be achieved in the most amazing – and sometimes alarming – ways. Sexual potency in a woman might, for example, be attained by placing some wormwood under the bed or by eating the pith of a pomegranate tree. It could be enhanced even more by wearing the right testicle of an ass in an amulet.

And bray all night long?

DOG'S BOLLOCKS

Aphrodisiacs also played an important role in the sex life of the Greeks – onions, crabmeat and snails were highly regarded – and these were still in fashion in the Middle Ages in many European countries. The mandrake was famed for its powers (which were said to derive from its phallic shape) as was the orchis plant. G. Rattray Taylor explains the amusing reason why in *Sex in History* (1953):

> The root of the orchis, which was thought to resemble the

testicles, as its popular name 'Dog Stones' shows, was eaten to induce fertility – though it was important to eat only that one of the stones which was hard, the soft one having a contrary effect. By the complementary argument, apparently, nuns used to eat the roots of the lily, or the nauseous *agnes castus*, to ensure chastity!

MADAME'S LITTLE FAVOURITE

The variety of aphrodisiacs is almost endless – from the use of pigeon droppings and snail excrement apparently popular in medieval England to dolphin's testicles which are still much fancied by the Japanese today. The Chinese emperors of the past, who often had dozens of wives and concubines, were sustained by a mixture of tea and sheep's eyelids *rubbed on the penis*; while in Germany in the eighteenth century, menstrual blood added to any drink was said to have the desired effect. The Cubeo tribe in Brazil believed that the penis and scrotum of a defeated enemy are particularly potent when presented to their wives – who must eat them to enhance their fertility – although their neighbours in Peru are happier to settle for the rather more mundane chilli and hot spices. Perhaps, though, the most revolting aphrodisiac of all has been reported by Alan Morrison in his *Noble Libertines* (1958):

> As Madame de Montespan, the mistress of the French King Louis XIV, grew older she tried any number of measures to retain his favour. When exotic costumes and cosmetics failed her, she turned to aphrodisiacs. If the records are to be believed, her most alarming endeavour was to slip toad excrement into one of the Sun King's favourite dishes . . .

A TIP WORTH TAKING

In his book *Women A-Z* (1961), Jean Jerome Romanet lists the following items as 'possessing the property of exciting sexual desire'. 'Swallow oysters (phosphorus), drink tea (caffeine), nibble asparagus (suggestive). Add a pinch of Spanish fly, if you like, or Alexandrian *ymbihine* from the beloved object, but don't count too much on it . . .'

'MEANS TO STIFFEN THE PENIS'

A little pamphlet entitled *Means to Stiffen the Penis* – attributed, doubtfully, to Galen – was a huge underground seller in eighteenth- and nineteenth-century Britain. It contained a wide-ranging list of aphrodisiacs under various headings: food and drink, drugs, potions and lotions and mechanical devices. The volume reiterated the advice of Martial (c. AD 40–104) in his *Epigrams* that 'wood pigeons check and blunt the manly power; let him not eat this bird who wishes to be amorous' and instead recommended the consumption of pepperwort (*Satureia*) to engender desire. Alternatively the seed of nettles (again!) could be mixed with pepper itself, or else take draughts of old wine into which powdered *pyrethrum* (a sort of chrysanthemum) had been stirred. These two remedies were known as 'fanning the fires of love'. The *Means to Stiffen the Penis* also detailed two recipes for super-sex it claimed had been used since the days of the ancient Greeks:

> In order to perform the coitus many times, take fifty pine-kernels in two glasses of wine, add powdered pepper to it, and drink . . .

> If you want to have a truly powerful erection, take honey, add powdered pepper to it, and smear it upon your *soles* . . .

Pepper certainly seems to be the spice of sex!

THE SCANDAL OF CHOCOLATE

Isaac Disraeli (1776–1848) who, in his time, was well known for his literary illustrations of people and history, is today perhaps best remembered as the father of the great English statesman and prime minister, Benjamin Disraeli. Yet Disraeli *père*'s series, *Curiosities of Literature*, published between 1791 and 1834, were a constant topic of conversation in society and his opinions were often as fascinating as they were controversial. Take this amusing comment on chocolate as an aphrodisiac:

> The immoderate use of chocolate in the seventeenth century was considered as so violent an inflamer of passions, that J.F. Rauch published a treatise against it and enforced the necessity of forbidding the monks to drink it. He added that if such an interdiction had already existed, that scandal with which the holy order had been branded might have proved more groundless.

THE SMELL ON HER BREATH

In a book entitled *The Ideal Marriage* (1960), a Dutch gynaecologist, T.H. Van de Velde, devoted a section to sexually stimulating foods, and included those which resembled sex organs (celery, asparagus, onions, etc.) as well as eggs and caviar (fish eggs). He also had this curious observation to make: 'After coitus, there is an unmistakable odour of semen on a woman's breath . . .'

FERTILE GROUND FOR QUESTIONS . . .

The existence of curious beliefs among people about fertility and conception were evident in the popular weekly column, 'The Family Doctor', which appeared in the British magazine *Lucky Star* during the first half of this century. Among the most curious questions on which the good doctor was asked to pronounce were:

* If wearing the hat of a Morris dancer could lead to pregnancy . . .
* If drinking vinegar while pregnant would cause the baby to be a boy . . .
* And whether the child of a married woman who had already had sex with other men could look like a former lover . . .

THE GIANT'S ERECTION

One of the most imposing fertility symbols in Britain is the naked chalk giant at Cerne Abbas in Dorset. Authorities are divided as to whether the 180-foot high figure carved into the hillside represents the hero-god Hercules – whose cult may have been brought to this country by early settlers from the Mediterranean – or if he is a Celtic god once worshipped by local tribes. In any event, a local tradition claims that a woman who makes love on the giant's erect phallus is sure to conceive. A newspaper report from the *Daily Telegraph* in 1980 tells of an audacious plan for the giant:

> Controversy has arisen in Dorset over the plans of a local sculptor to carve a female figure alongside the Cerne Abbas giant. Not so much about the idea, but the suggestion as to *who* the model for the giantess should be. Local residents have objected to the idea she should resemble Marilyn Monroe because the star was American and prefer the local-born sex symbol, Fiona Richmond.

SEX IN PARADISE

Adam and Eve have a lot to answer for because of their high jinks with an apple in the Garden of Eden. Obviously, things were very different before the first man fell for his partner's unadorned charms – but quite *how* different has provoked a great deal of speculation. Doctor G.F. Girdwood, a Victorian GP, seems to have been reflecting the disgust at the sexual and reproductive process that was felt by many people of his time when he wrote to *The Lancet* in 1852: 'It is my belief that in Paradise, human beings reproduced asexually. Only when man had fallen in the Garden of Eden was perfection replaced by the evil of sex.'

Well, if that doesn't take the pip . . .

MAKING THE MOULD

An alternative method of procreation was suggested in the sixteenth century by the German religious reformer Martin Luther (1483–1546). Famous for the civil disorder his ideas generated and the frequent burning of his books, Luther could still manage a little humour, as he shows in this instance from one of his sermons: 'The reproduction of mankind is a great marvel and mystery. Had God consulted me in the matter, I should have advised him to continue the generation of the species by fashioning them in clay.'

A model answer, surely.

PLANTING FOR TOMORROW

Sir Thomas Browne (1605–82) was a doctor and author who ran a large medical practice during the Civil War and still found time to reflect on various aspects of sex and morality. His books were a mixture of learning and quaint humour like *The Garden of Cyrus* (1658) which aimed to show that the number five pervades all plant life, and *Pseudodoxia Epidemica, or Enquiries into Vulgar and Common Errors* (1646) in which he makes the following comic observation:

> I could wish that there were any way to perpetuate the world without this trivial and vulgar way of coition. It is the foolishest act a wise man commits in his whole life. Nor is there anything that will deject his cold imagination more, when he shall consider what an odd and unworthy piece of folly he hath committed.

I speak not in any prejudice, nor am adverse from that sweet sex, but am naturally amorous of all that is beautiful. I can look a whole day with delight upon a handsome picture, though it is but of a tree. I only wish that we might procreate like trees, without conjunction.

Just like little acorns?

A SUCCESSFUL RIDE

A number of eighteenth-century quack doctors used the sexual size and strength of horses – stallions, in particular – as a means of promoting completely useless lotions for sale to childless women. Hand in glove (sometimes in the same sealed package) went pornographic pictures of unorthodox positions in which to have sex that were claimed would help females conceive – and again many of these used equine associations. Take this claim by the notorious Samuel Solomon, who promoted his 'knowledge' of sexual matters and his dubious products in *An Account of that Most Excellent Medicine, The Cordial Balm of Gilead* (1821): 'A certain

lady of quality in this country makes no scruple to say in company that she could not be got with child without riding St. George.'

England's great hero coming to the rescue again!

IMMACULATE CONCEPTION – 1

A young couple who never actually met are credited with the strangest conception on record. The event, which predates artificial insemination by over a century, occurred during the American Civil War, and was reported in the *American Weekly* of 4 November 1874:

> During an affray on May 12 between part of Ulysses S. Grant's army and a Confederate detachment, a soldier suddenly staggered and fell to the ground. At the same time a piercing cry was heard in a house nearby. Examination of the wounded soldier showed that a bullet had passed through his scrotum and carried away the left testicle. The same bullet had apparently penetrated the left side of the abdomen of a young lady, mid-way between the umbilicus and the anterior spinous process of the ileum and become lost in the abdomen. The young lady suffered an attack of peritonitis, but recovered.
>
> Two hundred and seventy eight days after the reception of the bullet, the young lady was delivered of a fine boy, weighing eight pounds, to the surprise of herself and the mortification of her parents and friends. After hearing of the bullet wound, the doctor concluded that the same ball had carried away the testicle of the young man and had penetrated the ovary of the young lady, and, with some spermatozoa upon it, had impregnated her. With this conviction, he approached the young man and told him of the circumstances. The soldier appeared sceptical at first, but consented to visit the young mother. A friendship ensued which soon ripened into a happy marriage . . .

IMMACULATE CONCEPTION – 2

A perhaps even stranger case of pregnancy occurring without intercourse taking place occurred in Greece in the sixteenth century. It was reported by a physician, Amatus Lusitanus, and concerned a Turkish woman living in Salonika who was bisexual: 'This woman, fresh from carnal connection with her husband, had a lesbian relationship with another woman. As a result, the second woman, a widow living on her own, became pregnant and nine months later was delivered of a baby girl.'

BABIES WITH TAILS

The eccentric eighteenth-century Scottish judge Lord James Monboddo (1714–99) was fascinated by the world of animals. For years he combined his profession at the bar with writing a six-volume work, *Origin and Progress of Language* (1773–92), in which he outlined his theories about human affinity with monkeys. Although this work can be seen as a forerunner of the modern science of anthropology, he was not above making the occasional outlandish suggestion, such as this one in 1785: 'All babies are born with tails. There is a conspiracy of silence among all midwives who cut them off at birth. Although I have been present at the birth of each of my own seven children, at each confinement the midwife outwitted me and destroyed the evidence!'

TAKE ONE SIDE OR THE OTHER

For almost a century a strange manuscript entitled *Mysteries of Nature Concerning the Generation of Man and the Voluntary Choice in the Sex of the Progeny* by one Dr P.F. Sixt of Erfurt in Germany lay forgotten. In 1870, a copy was found in New York and published with an introduction by another GP, Dr E. Trall, who claimed to have 'tested and satisfied himself' of the truth of Dr Sixt's claims. The most significant points were these:

* That the organs of the right side, in both sexes, are masculine, so to speak, and those on the left side, feminine.
* The secretion of one side cannot fertilise the ovum from the opposite side.
* Only when the opposite elements from the same side meet can there be any offspring.

MOTHER POWER

In 1876, a French doctor, M.A. Debay, claimed in his book *La Venus Féconde* that it was the female alone who was responsible for the sex of her child. After publishing the book, the unfortunate doctor was apparently hounded from his Paris surgery by outraged male patients and never heard of again. Debay declared in his now extremely rare work:

> It is the mother only who determines the sex of her offspring by a species of physiological discipline. From an analysis of the ovum, I have concluded that the whole question rests with it – the male element merely fertilising.
>
> I consider that each ovum contains a male and female principle, and that one or other of these predominates according to the temperament of the mother. If she be very effeminate, the ovum will have the female element in excess and will result in a girl. If the mother be something of a virago or of a masculine temperament, the male element will prevail and produce a corresponding result. A woman may therefore by transforming her own organization [sic] affect the sex of her offspring . . .

THE SEX LIES IN THE DIET

Another nineteenth-century French physician, Charles Girou de Buzareingues, attracted a lot of attention and a number of devoted followers to his theory that it was their ages and how much food men and women ate which decided the sex of their children. This extraordinary man, who lived and worked on a remote farm in Normandy, used both animals and local people to test his theory. A contemporary account describes it with ill-concealed mirth:

> Curious indeed are the experiments of Mr. Charles Girou de Buzareingues concerning the procreation of the sexes. He is led to believe that the sex depends upon the comparative vigour of the parents. To obtain an excess of female offspring the father should be young and ill-fed, while the mother should be of mature years and highly fed. The order should apparently be reversed to produce males.

Sounds like making a meal out of it, to me.

THE ALTERNATE THEORIES

In his book *The Law of Sex* (1883), the no-nonsense Victorian medical authority George B. Starkweather lists a number of fallacies about fertility that were then in vogue. One he describes as the 'Alternate Theory' – that Nature makes all human ova either male or female and supplies masculine one month and feminine the next – and another the concept of 'Genital Superiority' which claims that 'the more passionate parent stamps the sex of the child'. He reserves special irony for a certain Dr Hough:

> Would it not be positive confusion if Nature has, as Dr. Hough maintains, given but six days, at most, per month, in which females can be conceived – and if in the last two or three of these they must be insufferable harridans; and to the males has allotted as many more days – on the first three of which shall be produced specimens as much too effeminate as the preceding ones were too masculine? Facts certainly do not corroborate this assumption by showing nearly one-half of the human race wrongly sexed!

THE PIN-UP METHOD

The power of a woman's imagination has long been cited as a way of ensuring the sex of a child. This tradition, which has been recorded for many centuries, says that during sex the female should think about some beautiful figure from history. The following lines, which are at least three hundred years old, were often slipped to young brides by their mothers just before their wedding:

A boy you wish? A beauteous boy behold,
With lips a cherry red, and locks of gold;
Like him for whom Alexis sighed of old.
If female fruit you rather covet, view
A heavenly Venus such as Titian drew.

A better option than 'Shut your eyes and think of England?', perhaps?

THE PATTER OF LARGE FEET

The women of Lancashire in England have a rather more down-to-earth tradition when it comes to selecting the sex of a child: "Tis a boy you want, then make your man come to bed wearing his boots.'
Curiously, there's no mention of his socks!

THE HEIGHT OF FASHION

Vivienne Westwood, the controversial fashion designer, presented an exploration into the relationship between art and fashion for Channel 4's series *Painted Ladies – Aesthetic Lust* in May 1996. During a sequence about the statues of the upstanding ancient Greek god Priape, she informed viewers: 'Previous generations used to chop off the penises from statues and keep them in the archives of museums. Some women used them for sexual purposes like dildos. I have even seen them used as paperweights.'

SACRIFICE AU DIEU PRIAPE
Gravé fur une Calcedoine.

A MARKET THAT LASTS ALL YEAR

The final word in this section on fertility and conception should, I think, be given to *Aristotle's Masterpiece*:

> I do caution the male from attempting too often to reiterate those amorous engagements till conception be confirmed. Even

then the husband should remember that it is a market that lasts all year and he should have a care of spending his stock too lavishly. Nor would his wife like him at all the worse for it. For women rather choose to have a thing done well than to have it often; and well and often too, can never hold out.

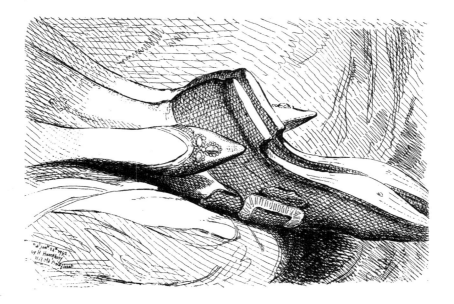

5.

THE
PRACTICE OF
PENILE
JOGGING

For hundreds of years – especially during the Victorian period and the early years of this century – masturbation was regarded as one of the curses of mankind. Scientists, doctors and even philosophers went hand in hand in regarding it as a disease and the cause of many diseases. Advice was given in the most forbidding tones about the dangers of indulging in self-relief – 'penile jogging', one more recent satirist has called it – and a variety of bizarre and comic devices were invented to counter the practice. For a period of two hundred years lasting well into the twentieth century, a dogma known as 'The Doctrine of Masturbatory Insanity' dominated Western society, as this next section will reveal.

Interestingly, though, in the earliest mentions of masturbation it was regarded in quite the opposite way. Take, for example, the Greek philosopher Diogenes (412–323 BC). This old man, famous for having taken up residence in a barrel and living the most austere and ascetic existence, regarded the practice as a means for sexual relief. He proclaimed defiantly with all the conviction of a man who *knew*: 'I wish to heaven that I could satisfy my hunger when my stomach barks for food by rubbing it . . .'

JUST RUB IT BETTER . . .

That font of knowledge, the Greek physician Galen of Pergamon, went further and actually recommended masturbation – especially for women. In his case, though, it had to be administered *by* the doctor to his female patients for the relief of what he called 'hysteria'. Galen explains:

> Following the warmth of the remedies, and arising from the touch of the genital required by this treatment, there follow twitchings accompanied at the same time by pain and pleasure, after which the women emit turbid and abundant sperm, and from that time on are freed of all the evil they feel . . .

IT'S NO SIN

A veteran Roman soldier, Albius Tibullus, who lived during the first century AD, argued that it was no sin if any of the wives of his troops masturbated while the men were away fighting. Tibullus, who apparently preferred writing poetry and debating philosophical matters to making war, understood the strains put on a marriage when the husband was absent and counselled his readers:

* That women undergo emotion or wetting through desire for their absent husband . . .
* They desire the same experience out of love as men . . .
* They may excite the process manually, provided that they refer the act to the absent husband . . .

Problem was, the post took even longer in Roman times!

A DANGEROUS ALLUREMENT

Right up to the seventeenth century, masturbation seems to have been generally regarded in a favourable light, if the evidence of the few surviving medical texts is to be believed. In one curious work, *Hippolytus Redivivus*, published during that time, the anonymous author came up with another reason why masturbation was particularly good for men. He wrote: 'Be it well known that this practice is well thought of in some quarters as a remedy against the dangerous allurements of women.'

O N A N I A;

OR, THE

H E I N O U S S I N

OF

𝕾𝖊𝖑𝖋-𝕻𝖔𝖑𝖑𝖚𝖙𝖎𝖔𝖓.

A N D

All its Frightful Confequences, in both SEXES, Confider'd,

WITH

Spiritual and Phyfical Advice to thofe, who have already injur'd themfelves by this abominable Practice.

And feafonable Admonition to the *Youth* of the Nation, (of both SEXES) and thofe whofe Tuition they are under, whether *Parents, Guardians, Mafters,* or *Miftreffes.*

The EIGHTH EDITION, Corrected, and Enlarg'd to almoft as much again, as particulariz'd at the End of the P R E F A C E; and are all the ADDITIONS, that will be made to this BOOK, how often foever it may come to be Reprinted.

And ONAN *knew that the Seed fhould not be his: and it came to pafs, when he went in unto his Brothers Wife, that he fpilled it on the Ground, left that he fhould give Seed to his Brother. And the Thing which he Did, difpleafed the* LORD: *wherefore he Slew him alfo.* GEN. 38, ver. 9. 1c.

L O N D O N: Printed by ELIZ. RUMBALL, for THOMAS CROUCH, Bookfeller, at the *Bell* in *Pater-Nofter-Row,* near *Cheapfide,* 1723. [Price Stitch'd Two Shillings.]

THE RISE OF SELF-ABUSE

The book which is generally credited with having started the hysteria about masturbation was the work of an eighteenth-century clergyman turned quack doctor. Very little else is known about this anonymous figure who in 1710 published a high-sounding volume entitled *Onania; Or, the Heinous Sin of Self-Pollution and All its Frightful Consequences in both Sexes Considered.* The reverend gentleman behind the work threatened fire and brimstone to all those who abused themselves – at the same time offering a patent medicine at half a sovereign a box which would remedy the 'heinous sin'. There is evidence that the book ran into many editions – though no word as to how well or otherwise the medicine sold – but it certainly invented a bogy that was to haunt mankind. The author summed up the fate that awaited all 'self-pollutors' in these words: 'If we turn our eyes on licentious Masturbators, we shall find them with meagre Jaws and pale Looks, with feeble Hams and legs without Calves, their generative faculties weakened if not destroyed in the Prime of their Years. A Jest to others and a Torment to themselves.'

THE SOLITARY ORGASM

The first genuine medical man to support the English clergyman's claims about the sins of Onania – *coitus interruptus* – was a Swiss physician, Samuel Tissot (1718–97), who wrote what would become the 'classic' work on the subject. *L'Onanisme: Dissertation sur les Maladies Produites par la Masturbation* in 1760. He was obviously a man worried about *all* sexual activity, having written earlier that it was dangerous because 'it causes blood to rush to the brain which in turn starves the nerves, making them more likely to damage and therefore increasing the likelihood of insanity'. Self-abuse, 'the solitary orgasm', was, though, by far the worst kind of sexual activity and he devoted over three hundred pages to explaining just why in the most lurid terms. Despite this, the occasional voice of sanity could be heard – though the evidence suggests such people were completely ignored. Take the writer who aptly called himself 'Philocastitatus' (and was in all probability a physician) who published a pamphlet two years later, *Onania Examined and Detected; Or, The Error, Impertinence*

and Contradiction of a Book called Onania *Discovered and Exposed* and in which he delivered this wicked summation of the clergyman: 'When our author says that he cannot help thinking that Such Persons Who Delay Marriage after such a Time, must be naturally impotent or rendered so by some vicious practice – I am persuaded the Reader needs no interpreter to explain what has been the Author's own Frailty or Infirmity . . .'

SOMETHING TO REMEMBER?

The man generally credited with being the 'father of American psychiatry', Benjamin Rush (1746–1813), was also a fanatical opponent of masturbation. Although widely regarded as the leading physician of his time, Rush was not above recommending bloodletting or scourging as a cure for self-abuse. Writing in *Medical Inquiries and Observations upon Disease of the Mind* (1812), he thundered: 'Masturbation produces seminal weakness, impotence, dysury, tabes dorsalis, pulmonary consumption, dyspepsia, dimness of sight, vertigo, epilepsy, hypochondriasis, managlia, fatuity, death and loss of memory . . .'

A POX ON THE WORLD

Even such an inflammatory statement pales in comparison with the views of an American surgeon aptly named Alfred Hitchcock, who blamed much of the illness in the nation on onanism. He claimed to have seen a 23-year-old man die 'after six years of habitual masturbation', and in a letter to the *New Orleans Medical and Surgical Journal* in 1842 warned all his fellow physicians: 'Neither plague, nor war, nor smallpox, nor a crowd of similar evils, have resulted more disastrously for humanity than the habit of masturbation: it is the destroying element of civilised society.'

THE ROAD TO RUIN

The chronicler of nineteenth-century prostitution, William Acton, was also a dedicated opponent of masturbation, as he revealed in his book *Functions and Disorders of the Reproductive Organs in Youth* (1857). From the time of King Solomon to the present day, he said, this kind of 'unmitigated evil' had led to a terrible end and continence was the key: 'voluntary and entire forbearance from sexual excitement or indulgence in any form'. The passions had to be controlled with 'a steady hand' (sic), said Acton, and the best remedy was 'the shock of cold water falling on the organs which in susceptible people is most beneficial'. But if none of this had any effect:

> Let us now notice the symptoms when a boy has been incontinent. In extreme cases the outward signs of debasement are only too obvious. The frame is stunted and weak, the muscles undeveloped, the eye is sunken and heavy, the complexion is sallow, pasty, or covered with spots of acne, the hands are damp and cold and the skin moist. His intellect becomes sluggish and enfeebled, and if his evil habits are persisted in he may end in becoming a drivelling idiot or a peevish valetudinarian. The simple truth is that the wear and tear of the nervous system arising from the incessant excitement of sexual thoughts and the large expenditure of semen has exhausted the vital force of the incontinent, and has reduced the immature frame to a pitiable wreck.

Acton added that there was just one exception to the rule 'that no man may by any unnatural means cause the expulsion of semen':

> On the other hand, the occasional occurrence of nocturnal emissions or wet dreams is quite comparable with, and indeed is expected as a consequence of continence, whether temporary or permanent . . .

AMATORY VERTIGO

The lugubrious Professor Orson Fowler was, not surprisingly, much exercised by the dangers of self-abuse in his *Sexual Science* (1870), pointing out that there was other physical evidence even more obvious than Acton had described:

> Stance is another sign. Self-polluters often stand and sit in the posture assumed during masturbation. They also often carry

their hands to the private parts, and in laughing they throw this part of their bodies forward . . .

Fowler also believed that the act 'if practised before puberty, dwarfs and enfeebles the sexual organs', corrupted the morals, and endangered the soul's salvation. He had a particular word of warning for young women:

If practised in girlhood, does it affect married life? Yes, those girls who practise it fail to develop as women. They become flat-chested and lose the female glow which draws gentlemen around them. They develop amatory vertigo and become very nervous . . .

THE SERIAL EFFECTS

The American John Harvey Kellogg, from whose Battle Creek Sanitarium emerged the first popular breakfast foods that still bear his name, claimed that many other attitudes in young men and women could be attributed to masturbation, including 'fickleness, bashfulness, unnatural boldness, being easily frightened, aversion to girls in boys but a decided liking for boys in girls, bad position in bed, a fondness for eating unnatural and hurtful or irritating articles such as salt, pepper, spices, vinegar, mustard, clay, slate pencils, plaster and chalk, biting the fingernails, the use of obscene words and phrases' and so on almost *ad infinitum*. Kellogg's book *Plain Facts for Old and Young* (1882) has since been accused of inculcating in vast numbers of Americans the idea that masturbation led to insanity, and also of adding to the misinformation about menstruation and the 'morbid influences and serious derangements' of which young women should beware. In it he wrote:

There is no doubt that many young women have permanently injured their constitutions while at school by excessive mental taxation during catamenial periods, to which they were prompted by ambition to excel, or were compelled by the 'cramming system' too generally pursued in our schools and particularly in young ladies' seminaries.

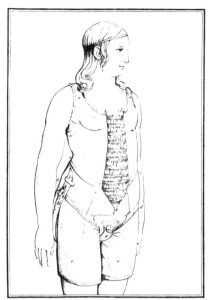 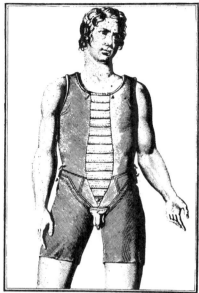

MEASURING UP TO THE JOB

Allen W. Hagenbach was a doctor in Chicago, USA, who in 1842 studied over eight hundred male inmates at Cook County Hospital said to be 'insane' from self-abuse. Later he wrote an essay, *Insanity and Death from Masturbation*, intended, he said, 'to counteract the exaggerated statements of the charlatans and those popular works designed to excite fears for mercenary ends or show the practice as harmless'. As part of his research, Hagenbach had got to the very core of the matter:

> I have measured the genitalia of 26 insane masturbators and it is true to say that the penis of such masturbators is, in general terms, enormously enlarged . . . Among them were also three with atrophied appendages. One of these insane masturbators,

an effeminate young man, was unwilling to make any efforts at reform, despite my best efforts. He carried everywhere with him a fan and did needlework.

A LITTLE LEARNING . . .

A nineteenth-century French doctor, Dr X. Bourgeois, also did research among 'sufferers' in a number of institutions in his country and reported in a book, *The Passions in Their Relations to Health and Diseases* (1873), that he had concluded that habitual masturbation was traceable to several causes – but three in particular: 'There are many causes, it is true, but among these must be highlighted the "sensual education" in schools, the use of aphrodisiac foods, and occupations that require prolonged sitting.'

A JERK IN THE HAND . . .

The great American satirist Mark Twain (1835–1910) poked fun at many entrenched institutions and traditions in his essays, and it is perhaps not surprising to find that masturbation – especially the belief that it caused illness – should have caught his interest. In a hilarious address, 'Some Remarks on the Science of Onanism', delivered to the 'Stomach Club' in Paris in 1879, he debunked the whole idea by satirising its therapeutic powers. As a matter of record, Twain's words were considered so scandalous at the time that almost a century passed before they first appeared in print . . .

> Homer in the second book of the *Iliad* says with fine enthusiasm, 'Give me masturbation or give me death!' Caesar in his *Commentaries* says, 'To the lonely it is company; to the forsaken it is a friend; to the aged and to the impotent it is a benefactor; they that are penniless are yet rich, in that they still have this majestic diversion.' In another place this experienced observer has said, 'There are times when I prefer it to sodomy.'
> Robinson Crusoe says, 'I cannot describe what I owe to this

gentle art.' Queen Elizabeth said, 'It is the bulwark of Virginity.' Cetewayo, the Zulu hero, remarked, 'A jerk in the hand is worth two in the bush.' The immortal Franklin has said, 'Masturbation is the mother of invention.' He also said, 'Masturbation is the best policy.'

Michelangelo and all the other old masters – Old Master, I will remark, is an abbreviation, a contraction – have used similar language. Michelangelo said to Pope Julius II, 'Self-negation is noble, self-culture is beneficent, self-possession is manly, but to the truly grand and inspiring soul they are poor and tame compared to self-abuse.'

A PASSION FOR LIFE

One body of men very active in Victorian England trying to put an end to masturbation among young boys was the Social Purity Alliance, a high-minded group of former public school pupils led by the Honourable Edward Lyttelton. In 1887, they published – 'For Private Circulation Only' – Lyttelton's *The Causes and Prevention of Immorality in Schools*, in which the author warned:

> The least defilement by hand enormously increases the difficulties of continence in manhood when masturbation may become the one absorbing and uncontrollable passion of life . . .

> The precocious indulgence of boyhood may, as the ungovernable passion of manhood, become responsible for the support of prostitution . . .

TOP TWENTY HITS

The American psychologist and educator Granville Stanley Hall (1846–1924), who initiated the child-study movement in the US with his ground-breaking book *The Contents of Children's Minds on Entering School* (1894), also compiled a very curious list of the causes of masturbation, which he described as 'one of the most morbid forms of sex perversion'. His 'Top Twenty Causes' appeared in *Adolescence*, published in 1904:

* Springtime
* Warm Climates
* Improper Clothes
* Indigestion
* Nervousness
* Defective Cleanliness
* Prolonged Standing
* Monotonous Walking
* Sitting Cross-legged
* Perfume
* Spanking
* Corsets
* Late Rising
* Feather Beds
* Straining the Memory
* Playing Solitude
* Rocking Chairs
* Horseback Riding
* Bicycles
* Pockets

The origin of 'pocket billiards' no doubt . . .

A CASE OF MORTON'S FORK

There is little doubt that many Victorian doctors who encountered cases of female masturbation were shocked. They believed – in the words of one of their colleagues who shall remain anonymous – that it was 'irrelevant to a woman's feelings whether she had sex organs or not'. Where the 'problem' was admitted, though, there was only one answer: a clitoridectomy. R.A. Spitz explains the term in the *Yearbook of Psychoanalysis* (1953):

The credit for this discovery belongs to Isaac Baker Brown, a prominent London surgeon who later became the president of the Medical Society of London. He introduced Clitoridectomy around 1858 because he believed that masturbation caused hysteria, epilepsy and convulsive diseases. Sufferers were dealt with, as so often in this context, by Morton's Fork – those who admitted masturbating had revealed the cause; those who denied it were lying. One woman who had been castrated for the 'sexual perversion of masturbation' wrote back to her castrator to report: 'My condition is all I could desire. I know and feel that I am well. I never think of self-abuse: it is foreign and distasteful to me.'

THE DANGEROUS CLITORIS

Dr Samuel Ashwell, who was a lecturer at Guy's Hospital in London at this same period, also thundered on about the dangers of masturbation and sexual passion, and especially the source of these problems, the clitoris. Enlarged clitorises in particular 'subdued every feeling of modesty and delicacy in a woman', Ashwell declared, 'leading to constant headaches and frequent attacks of hysteria'. There was only one course of action for this 'condition', the lecturer insisted in a speech given in 1844:

If the growth is insensible, and relief is sought for its mechanical annoyance, the best way is to excise it. Excision also is required when the growth is attended with undue sensibility. A few leeches may be applied near the part to eliminate sexual arousal, and Hydrocyanic acid in a solution will be found very efficacious as a lotion . . .

DOCTOR MOODIE'S GIRDLE

Scottish women were particularly prone to masturbation in the early nineteenth century, according to a cheerless little Edinburgh physician named John Moodie who styled himself 'MD and

Surgeon' and was responsible for inventing 'The Female Girdle of Chastity' in an attempt to stamp out the practice. Moodie was convinced that women who masturbated would become barren, and he was particularly alarmed at the example being set by 'Board School Misses' to their impressionable young female pupils. In his experience (sic) the practice was 'terribly prevalent and carried out not only digitally, but also with the help of the *godemiche*'. These objects, he said, were 'constantly in use' and it was more common for married women to have them than to be without. Even more alarming, mothers were teaching their girls how to use the devices, too! A description of Moodie's invention appears in E.J. Dingwall's *The Girdle of Chastity* (1931):

> The Moodie Girdle of Chastity consisted of a cushion made out of rubber or some other soft material and suitably covered with silk, linen or soft leather. This cushion or pad formed the base into which was fixed a kind of grating, and this part of the apparatus rested upon the vulva, the pad being large enough to press upon the *mons veneris*. The lower part of the pad rested upon the perineum, being curved so as to fit the parts to be enclosed. The bars of the grating were to be made of ivory or bone and were so arranged in the pad that when in position they pressed up against the *labia majora* opposite the vagina. The whole apparatus was affixed by means of belts to a pair of tight-fitting drawers and secured by a padlock, a secret flap being made so as to close over the key hole. Not only was this device an effective remedy against masturbation, declared Moodie, but also as a means of avoiding seduction it has a high and essential importance.

The original cast iron drawers, I'd call them!

WIRED FOR SAFETY – 1

The idea of infibulation – putting a silver wire through the foreskin to prevent masturbation – was first advocated by a

German physician, S.G. Vogel, as early as 1786. A century later, another German doctor, Manfred Boehn, refined the idea because he believed it would be 'an ideal way to stop impecunious bachelors from having offspring'. His instructions are excruciating enough to read, let alone put into action:

> The foreskin is drawn forward and gently compressed between a pair of perforated metal plates so that when a hollow needle, containing a core of lead wire, is stuck through it, it is hardly felt. When the wire has been drawn through, it is bent so that it cannot press on the adjacent parts. Both ends are now brought together and soldered together with a small soldering rod.
>
> As soon as the knot, the size of a pea, has cooled off, a solid object is held against it; a small metal seal is pressed on it and this is afterwards kept in safety. This makes it impossible to open the infibulation and afterwards close it without being discovered.

WIRED FOR SAFETY – 2

An American advocate of infibulation, Dr David Yellowless, advocated much the same treatment. In 1876 he wrote to the *Journal of Mental Science* about his work and the number of cases he had treated. He added with masterly understatement: 'The sensation among my patients will be of interest. I was struck by the conscience-stricken way in which they submitted to the operation on their penises. I mean to try it on a large scale and go on wiring all masturbators . . .'

THE AMERICAN REMEDY

According to a report in *The Lancet* in 1870, a considerable number of American doctors were then favouring a form of cauterisation to 'guard the penis against improper manipulation'.

This would result in a 'slight soreness of the body of the organ sufficient to render erection painful', the journal stated. If this failed, then there was always 'The American Remedy'. A description of this gruesome device is given in *The Shoals and Quicksands of Youth* by Dr Samuel Kahn, published the following year:

> 'The American Remedy' consists of a ring of common metal, with a screw passing through one of its sides, and projecting into the centre, where it has a button extremity for application to the part affected [the penis] at bedtime. Not only will this device alleviate temptation, but will prevent nocturnal emissions, and is being extensively used.

GUARDING AGAINST BAD WAYS

Mothers were constantly being reminded in the late nineteenth century to be on the look-out for the 'evil' of self-abuse among their children – even when they were little more than babies. The American author Emma Drake made a particular point of this in her book *What a Young Wife Ought to Know*, published in 1901:

> While yet very young, they can be taught that the organs are to be used by them only for throwing off the waste water in the system, but they are so closely related to other parts of the body, that handling them at all will hurt them and make them sick.
>
> Tell them that little children, sometimes when they do not know this, form the habit of handling themselves and as a result become listless and sick, or develop epileptic fits, and many times become idiotic and insane. This will so impress them, that they will not, properly guarded, fall easily into bad ways . . .

CLIMBING INTO TROUBLE

The indefatigable William Acton, who believed that violent exercise could help the schoolboy masturbator to keep his mind on purer things, warned in all seriousness of one particular activity that must be avoided:

> Several confessions that have been made to me induce the suggestion for the consideration of parents and schoolmasters, whether the practice of *climbing* in gymnasia is not open in some degree to objections? The muscles chiefly called into action in climbing are those, the excessive exertion of which, tends to excite sexual feelings. Boys have, as I know, sometimes discovered this, for more than one adult has told me that, when at school, he had found that he derived pleasure from the exercise, and had repeated it quite in ignorance of the consequences!

NO BALLS AT ALL

One of the horrifying methods prescribed in the 1880s in America by certain medical men to stem what they saw as the 'tide of masturbation' then sweeping the country, was to lop off the testicles of 'sufferers'. In March 1884, the *Boston Medical and Surgical Journal* reported a typical example of this kind of operation and quoted one of the surgeons involved, a Dr J. Crosby:

> Believing that removing the testicles will remove the great source of difficulty, masturbation, I recommend castration, with the confident expectation that it will prove successful. One man I treated recently was so miserable, and life had become such a burden to him, that he was not only willing to submit to the operation, but urged me to perform it, which I did . . .
>
> He has now the appearance of good health, is cheerful and happy. He also has every prospect of good health, a life of

usefulness, and can walk miles with as much ease and elasticity as anyone . . .

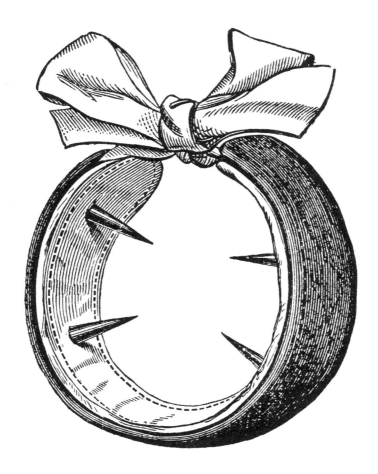

NOCTURNAL RINGING

Many bizarre devices were manufactured to prevent young people from masturbating in the Victorian era – including a range of leather strait-jackets, constricting rubber appliances of one sort or another, and pairs of gloves made from abrasive wire gauze material. Boys could always be fitted with clamps which painfully prevented the penis from becoming erect, or attached to an electrical appliance that rang a bell and alerted parents or

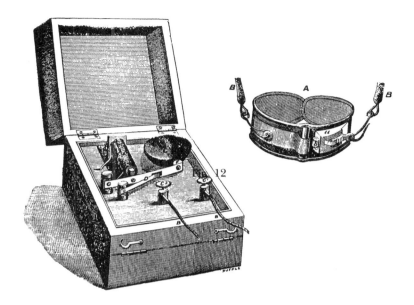

guardians to any nocturnal activities. *In extremis*, there was even the idea of one C.D.W. Colby for 'A Mechanical Restraint of Masturbation in Young Girls' which he presented in the *New York Medical Record* in 1897:

> Such girls should be forced to sleep in sheepskin pants and jacket made into one garment, with their hands tied to a collar about the neck. The feet must be tied to the footboard and by a strap about the waist fastened to the headboard, so that they may not slide down the bed and use their heels. In the case of those girls who resist all reason, they must be wholly encased by a physician in canvas and splints.

SPIKED IN THE NICK OF TIME

Just how widespread the use of these anti-abuse measures became during Queen Victoria's reign – not to mention how uncomfortable and unpleasant they were – may be judged from this comment by Alex Comfort in his book *The Anxiety Makers* (1967):

One is inclined at first sight to put such things to the account of sexual fantasy, until one realises that even adults were counselled by William Acton to adopt the 'common practice' of sleeping with the hands tied, or by J.L. Milton of the Hospital for Diseases of the Skin to make use of a locked chastity belt. Spontaneous emissions, too, were dangerous to health if frequent, and called for the wearing of spiked or toothed rings to awaken the sleeper, or an electric bell on the principle of the modern enuresis alarm, if healthy outdoor hobbies like botany failed to subdue the flesh.

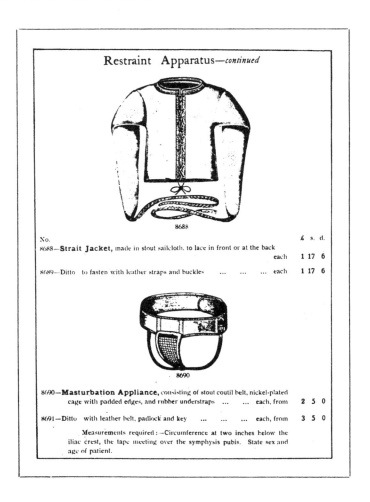

Restraint Apparatus—*continued*

8688

No.   £   s.   d.
8688—**Strait Jacket,** made in stout sailcloth, to lace in front or at the back
                                                                            each   1 17   6

8689—Ditto to fasten with leather straps and buckles   ...   . each   1 17   6

8690

8690—**Masturbation Appliance,** consisting of stout coutil belt, nickel-plated
        cage with padded edges, and rubber understraps ...   ... each, from   2   5   0

8691—Ditto with leather belt, padlock and key   ...   . each, from   3   5   0

          Measurements required : —Circumference at two inches below the
          iliac crest, the tape meeting over the symphysis pubis. State sex and
          age of patient.

THE SINS OF THE FATHERS

Sylvanus Stall, as his name suggests, could have stepped straight from the pages of a Victorian novel: stiff in his views about society and morals. He was indeed an archetypal Victorian Doctor of Divinity – not, it must be pointed out, of medicine, though he was much admired by many doctors – with a self-appointed mission to warn young people about the perils of masturbation. His good works (of which there were dozens) were not only translated into various languages including Dutch, French and Swedish, even Japanese and Urdu, but also issued on phonograph cylinders. In one of them, *What a Young Boy Ought to Know* (1897), Stall – a 'champion moral blackmailer' as he has since been called – warned that the dangers of self-abuse had far-reaching implications. Almost unbelievably far-reaching:

> But the consequences which result from masturbation do not stop with the boy who practises it, nor with his parents, brothers and sisters, friends and relatives, but where such a boy lives to become a man, if he marries, and should become a father, his children after him must suffer to some measurable degree the results of his sin. As in grain, so in human life, if the quality of the grain which is sown in the field is poor, the grain that grows from it will be inferior.
>
> When a boy injures his reproductive powers, so that when a man his sexual secretion shall be of an inferior quality, his offspring will show it in their physical, mental and moral natures. So you see that even a young boy may prepare the way to visit upon his children that are to be, the results of vices and sins committed long years before they were born. This surely is a very impressive thought!

So take yourself in hand, you can almost hear Stall insisting from the phonograph . . .

THE MALE CHASTITY BELT

San Francisco in 1897 was still a part of the old Wild West where men were men and women . . . were in short supply. Yet it is in this unlikely locality that a certain Michael McCormick invented a device to prevent masturbation, stop involuntary nocturnal seminal emissions, and, curiously, 'to control waking thoughts'. McCormick lodged the plans for his appliance – to all intents and purposes a male chastity belt – at the United States Patent Office on 10 August 1897. It consisted, he said, of 'a plate of any suitable material' which could be secured to the body and 'having an aperture through which the proper member is to be passed'. The specifications were as follows:

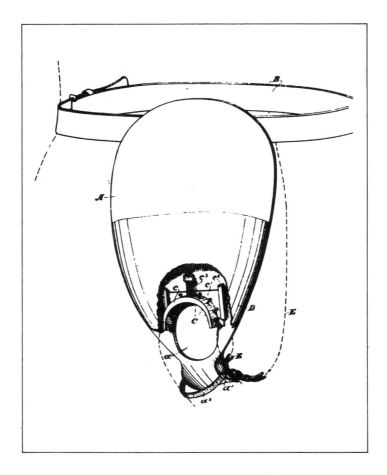

The device is adjusted to the person by fitting plate A over the abdomen and securing it by belt B. The organ is passed through the aperture a, which fits close up around the base, and this member is then drawn down and rests in lip a^1 and is secured lightly therein by the band or strip a^2. The pricking-points [sic] are adjusted so as to lie in such proximity above, though clear of, the organ, as may be found best.

The member, being drawn and held down in lip a^1, will, as long as there is no excitement, not be in contact with the pricking-points, and will be positively held clear thereof. Now when from any cause, expansion in the organ begins, it will come in contact with the pricking-points, and the necessary pain or warning sensation will result.

If the person be asleep or otherwise inattentive, he will be awakened or recalled to his senses in time to prevent further expansion. If he be asleep, an involuntary emission will be prevented by his awakening; or, if conscious, to divert his thoughts from lascivious channels. Voluntary self-abuse will be checked as the wearer will not take the trouble to relieve himself of the appliance and cannot continue his practice without removing it. An irresponsible wearer may have it permanently attached.

Patently absurd, some may call it.

CLAMPED AND CLUNKED!

Plans for another device to put a stop to self-abuse were handed in to the US Patent Office in 1906 by one Raphael Sonn of New York. Described innocuously as a 'Sanitary Appliance', it looked more like an instrument of medieval torture. Again the intention was the same as McCormick's device of a decade earlier. Constructed of lightweight metal – but without any form of padding – the details of the invention were as much to the point as its intention:

The 'Sanitary Appliance' is designed to discourage self-

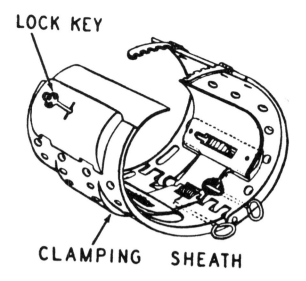

LOCK KEY

CLAMPING SHEATH

gratification. It consists of a sheath having clamping and gripping members which, upon erection of the male organ, close in and cause sharp pain until the mood passes.

Curiously, neither of these patents gave instructions what to do if, as seemed likely on occasions, emotions got the better of a wearer. That was left to a Dr R.F. Sturgis in his book *Treatment of Masturbation* (1910), which discussed a whole range of such ideas:

If the penis erects while the wearer is asleep and he is awakened by the jab of metal on flesh, he should first remove the device. Next, soak the organ in cold water until it has subsided, and once again affix the apparatus to the genitals. The wearer can then return to his innocent sleep, assured that a moral as well as a material victory has been gained!

GETTING TO THE BOTTOM OF BLACKHEADS

Sigmund Freud (1856–1939), the founder of psychoanalysis, also had a quirky view on masturbation, which he believed 'deserved more attention than it has hitherto received', according to a lecture he gave in 1898. He was obviously as good as his word and set about the research, because in 1915 he published *The Unconscious*, in which he described the particular case of one young man whose skin was covered in blackheads and the significance – he said – they had in the boy's life:

> He liked to evacuate these blackheads, a common enough practice among adolescents. Pressing out the contents of the blackheads is clearly to him a substitute for masturbation. The cavity which then appears owing to his fault, is the female genital, i.e., the fulfillment of the threat of castration (or the phantasy representing the threat) provoked by his masturbation.

A NOSE FOR TROUBLE

For several years, Freud was friendly with an eccentric young doctor, Wilhelm Fliess, who shared his interest in masturbation. Fliess, however, believed he had found a way of treating the cause, which he described as 'Nasal Reflex Neurosis'. In a word, he was convinced that it was the *nose* that caused, aggravated or actually controlled all sexual disorders – therefore by cutting off the offending proboscis, temptation could be removed. Perhaps not *all* the nose had to be done away with, as Fliess explained in 1902 just before his madcap scheme was outlawed by the medical profession:

> There are particular spots in the nose which relate to abdominal disorders. Treating one nasal spot, for example, will cure irregular menstruations. This may be achieved by cauterising the part or numbing it with cocaine.
>
> Women who masturbate are generally dysmenorrheal. They can only be cured through an operation on the nose if they do not give up this bad practice. In extreme cases, it may be necessary to extract the nasal bone altogether in order for them to recover perfect health . . .

IN THE PALM OF THE HAND . . .

A number of psychiatrists have subsequently followed Freud's lead and investigated the same areas of sexuality that fascinated him. One such man was an eccentric German, Dr Rudolf Friedman, who first became notorious in the early fifties when he suggested that the reason for Christ's aggression against his own mother was 'his unconscious did not believe her to be a virgin'. In 1954, in a paper which dealt extensively with masturbation, he pointed out another symptom which, despite being wholly imaginary, has since found a place in popular folklore: 'Note the long, thin, almost imperceptible black hair growing out of the middle of the palm of the left hand of masturbators.'

THE JOYS OF WATER

Among the many curious papers that have been written about female sexuality, the study by Eugene Halpert, 'On a Particular Form of Masturbation in Women: Masturbation with Water', enjoys a certain notoriety. Published in 1973 in the *Journal of the American Psychoanalytic Association*, Halpert described the activity as unusual and set out to explain 'why these particular women chose this solution to their unconscious conflicts'. His answer? *Penis envy.* He explained:

Women who masturbate by running water over their clitoris are using this form of masturbation to express the supplementary fantasies:

1. I have my father's penis and can urinate/ejaculate like a man, and
2. I am able to urinate and destroy/castrate with my powerful stream in revenge for castration.

USE IT, OR LOSE IT!

In recent years, of course, the clock has turned full circle from the days of Diogenes, and masturbation is now being promoted by many sexologists as therapeutic, 'because it teaches the concept of self-pleasuring in its broadest sense', according to a pair of such experts, Martin Weisberg and Bobbie Whitney, in a lecture they delivered in Los Angeles in 1980. It has also been seen as a 'performance art' in the US. In 1972, an artist, Vito Acconci, buried himself under a gallery floor and simulated self-gratification, complete with moans. He called the 'art' *Seedbed*. The last word, though, goes to Thomas Szasz in his book *The Myth of Psychotherapy* (1978):

> The sexologists Masters and Johnson promote masturbation because they think it is therapeutic – maritally as well as medically. Maritally, they claim, masturbation is indicated for fully half of the husbands and wives in America. Medically, it is indicated especially for women and old men. Women need to masturbate during menstruation because it sounds better than Excedrin. Old men need to masturbate to keep in shape sexually. Heeding the old saw, 'Use It, Or Lose It', Masters and Johnson prescribe a kind of penile jogging . . .

6.

LOVE
LOCKED IN

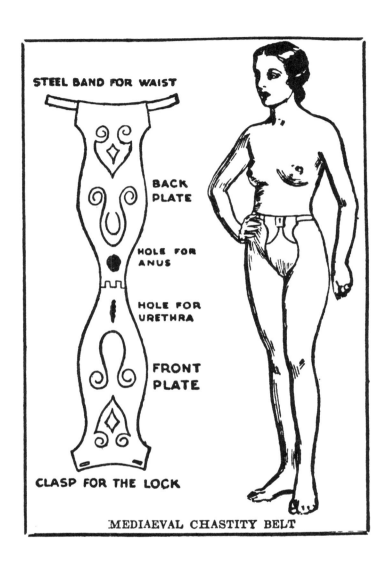

STEEL BAND FOR WAIST

BACK PLATE

HOLE FOR ANUS

HOLE FOR URETHRA

FRONT PLATE

CLASP FOR THE LOCK

MEDIAEVAL CHASTITY BELT

Among the many inventions that have been devised by the ingenuity of man to help – or hinder – sexual desire, the chastity belt is certainly the most famous. These lockable metal belts – *ceintures de chasteté*, as they are called – intended to prevent women from having sex in the absence of their husbands, have a curious history. The most popular theory of their origin claims they were introduced into Western Europe by the Crusaders returning from the East where they had been in service for many years. Apart from occasionally being affixed on the bodies of young boys during puberty, they were also employed, in a modified form, to guard against extramarital rear-entry copulation. Today, experts are agreed that the popular notion of the Crusaders using them to clunk-click their women while away at the wars is less likely than jealous husbands turning the key on predatory lovers.

The belts were often elegantly made in steel with a protective covering of polished ivory around the waist and genitals. Many girdles were trimmed with red velvet and decorated with beautifully artistic designs. One of the earliest illustrations of a chastity belt is to be found in a satirical German woodcut, dated 1590 (illustrated on page 142), which depicts a lady handing a large key to her husband while, behind a curtain, her lover is about to bribe the woman's maid for a spare! In recent times, these devices to lock love out have been used as items of decoration, while several manufacturers have even offered reproductions for sale in France, Britain and America. Chastity belts have also made the news in bizarre ways, as the following examples reveal:

> Police at Catania, Sicily, are investigating the case of a young Frenchwoman who was wearing an iron chastity belt which was so tight it had to be removed by doctors. Monique Michael,

25, said her Sicilian boyfriend, Paolo Butta, 40, forced her to wear the belt for a year because he was jealous. Butta denied he told the girl to wear the belt or that he was jealous . . . (*Daily Telegraph*, 29 December 1963)

*

Every morning the giant husband had to endure a humiliating ritual at the hands of his tiny wife. Before Gregory (36) was allowed to leave the house, 34-year-old Alexandra clamped a heavy leather chastity belt in place and padlocked it. When he got home at night, his jealous wife unlocked him so that he could relax in the bath. For 16 years Gregory wore the belt, and even though he was too ashamed to ask anyone for help, Alexandra changed the locks from time to time. But the ritual, which began 16 years earlier when Alexandra found her handsome husband dallying in a field with a blonde, ended suddenly when Gregory fell from his bicycle on his way to work. He broke both legs and when he was undressed in a village hospital near Durazzo, Albania, his secret was exposed. A doctor described the contraption as 'a very skilful piece of engineering which left Gregory certain freedom for bodily functions . . .' (*News of the World*, 5 January 1975)

*

Prince Charles has ordered a set of miniature chastity belts from an Essex firm for use as toilet paper holders. The firm had applied for a Royal Warrant . . . (*Time Out*, 6 February 1975)

*

As part of the opening ceremonies of a two-day Security and Safety Exhibition held at Vauxhall Holiday Park, Yarmouth, Mr. George Charlton, the Chief Constable of Norfolk, tried and failed to pick the lock of a chastity belt worn by Miss Nicole Wiseman, the shapely 19-year-old daughter of a police sergeant. 'I was a bit surprised when the job centre offered me two days' work modelling a chastity belt,' said Miss Wiseman, 'but it was good fun . . .' (*Yarmouth & Gorleston Advertiser*, 2 April 1981)

*

A wife forced to wear a chastity belt by her jealous husband has died from an infection caused by the rusty padlock. Police in Lima, Peru, said 22-year-old Rosa Esquen became ill after the lock on the tight leather belt dug into her flesh. They said her husband, Dionicio, had made the medieval-style belt out of thick, coarse rawhide. He locked the padlock and took the key with him when he went on business trips from their village. He was away on a trip when the infection set in and Rosa was dead by the time he returned. A state lawyer said Dionicio himself now faced up to five years locked up . . . (*The People*, 28 June 1987)

*

A chastity belt for men, based on a car steering wheel lock, is being snapped up by parents in Afghanistan to stop teenage sons chasing girls. The inventor, Inya Radyu, has named his device the 'Nub Club' . . . (*Sunday Mirror*, 21 July 1996)

THE GRAND CELESTIAL BED

James Graham (1745–94) has been described as 'the most inventive quack in British history' and certainly his 'Celestial Bed' is one of the most notorious sexual inventions in the annals of medicine. In 1779, this former Edinburgh medical student and travelling physician opened his 'Temple of Health' at Adelphi Terrace in London to give lectures and demonstrate his extraordinary invention, assisted by his 'Goddess of Health and of Hymen', a young lady in white silk robes and a rose-coloured girdle named Emma Lyons who would, in time, become Lady Hamilton and ultimately Lord Nelson's mistress.

The centrepiece of Graham's extravagant and ornamental 'Temple' dedicated to 'The Generation, Increase and Improvement of the Human Species' (entrance fee: two guineas) was 'The Grand Magnetico-Electric Celestial Bed', which he claimed was a guaranteed cure for sterility and the production of 'stronger, healthier and wiser children'. Measuring twelve feet by nine with twenty-eight pillars of glass, the bed was said to be modelled on that of 'the favourite Sultana in the Seraglio of the Grand Turk' and cost over £12,000 to build. Graham himself sat in a neighbouring room, beside a cylinder through which he passed to the bed chamber 'the electrical fire – that fluid which animates and vivifies all, and those cherishing vapours and oriental perfumes which I convey thither by means of glass'.

Temple of Health and of Hymen. Pall Mall.

THE LECTURE at the above place having been received by very numerous, polite and brilliant audiences of Ladies and Gentlemen with unbounded applause, it will be repeated This and every Evening this Week ; and precisely at 8 o'clock the Gentleman Usher of the Rosy Rod, assisted by the High Priestess, will conduct the rosy, the gigantic, the stupendous Goddess of Health to the Celestial Throne.

The blooming PRIESTESS of the TEMPLE will endeavour to entertain Ladies and Gentlemen of candour and good nature, by reading a Lecture on the simplest and most efficacious means of preserving health, beauty, and personal loveliness, and serene mental brilliancy, even to the extremest old age.

VESTINA, the GIGANTIC! on the Celestial Throne, as the Goddess of Health, will exhibit in her own person, a proof of the all-blessing effects of virtue, temperance, regularity, simplicity, and moderation ; and in these luxurious, artificial, and effeminate times, to recommend those great virtues.

The Temple (which exhibits more riches, more elegance, and more brilliancy than any royal Palace in the world) will as usual be sweetly illuminated with wax, in the highest, most dazzling, and most celestial magnificence from 7 till 10 o'clock, This evening and every Evening this week, and the Lecture will begin precisely at eight. Both before and after the Lecture, one of Vestina's Fairy Train will warble forth sweet celestial sounds.—*Admittance only* ONE SHILLING.

The magnificent Electrical Apparatus, and the supremely brilliant and *unique* decorations of this magical Edifice—of this enchanting Elysian Palace! where wit and mirth, love and beauty—all that can delight the soul, and all that can ravish the senses, will hold their court, This and every Evening this week, in chaste and joyous assemblage.

*** Ladies of rank and character are assured, that nothing will be said or seen, which can give even the smallest offence to the chastest and most delicate female eye or ear, and that every thing will be conducted with the most perfect decency and decorum.—Ladies are requested to come early, in order that they may be agreeably accommodated with seats.

*** A very few copies still remaining of Dr. Graham's Private Advisers (*sealed up, price One Guinea*) to those Ladies and Gentlemen who wish to have children, or to become snowy pillars of Health and Beauty, studded as it were with roses, and streaked with celestial blue, may now be had at only Half a Guinea ; his other curious and eccentric works, containing full descriptions of his Travels, Discoveries, Improvements, Principles, Cures, Electrical Apparatus, etc.—formerly 3s. 6d., now only 1s. 9d., and VESTINA, the rosy Goddess's warm Lecture, price 2s. 6d.

The 'scientific' argument behind Graham's device was that the fertilisation of the ovum is an electrical phenomenon, and the natural electricity created during sexual intercourse was artificially strengthened by the currents passing through the bed. Thousands of fashionable Londoners flocked to the 'Temple' (promoted in the press by advertisements such as the one reproduced on page 145) and it is recorded that on the three nights following its opening an average of nine hundred people were turned away. Those who did get to sleep in the bed with their partners – 'mostly young men who are rich and newly-arrived from the country with their mistresses', according to one report – enjoyed a mixture of vicarious pleasures and sensuality, if Graham's own description of it is to be believed:

The super-celestial dome of the bed containing the odiferous, balmy and aethereal spices, odours and essences, is coated on the underside with mirrors so disposed as to reflect the various charms and attitudes of the happy couple who repose in the bed in the most flattering, most luxurious and most enchanting style. The mattress is made from the tails of English stallions renowned for their sexual vigour and elastic in the highest degree. Below are fifteen hundredweight of magnets so arranged as to be continually pouring forth in an ever flowing circle powerful tides of the magnetic effluvium which every philosophic gentleman knows has a very strong affinity with the electric fire. As this aromatic, invigorating, springy mattress and the elastic magnets are pressed, the ardours of the transported pair are moderated, increased, or prolonged, by the corresponding music which flows or bursts forth from the pillars, from the dome, and from every part of the Elysium.

Sadly, the public's initial enthusiasm for 'The Celestial Bed' diminished as the claims for it foundered and in 1784 Graham was forced by his creditors to close the 'Temple'. Later, he tried unsuccessfully selling an 'Elixir of Life' for £1,000 a sample, advocated that Parliament should enact 'certain triennial or septiennial jubilees or matrimonial insolvency acts for the benefit of wretched, discordant and barren couples' and – despite all his earlier endeavours to promote sexual harmony – condemned what he described as 'the odious, indelicate and most harmful custom of man and wife continually pigging together in the same bed'. But perhaps the best of James Graham was to come last. In 1791, shortly before his death in poverty, he recruited a new Goddess of Health and instituted 'earth bathing' which was once more intended to promote sexual vigour. A newspaper report describes a typical demonstration:

> The Doctor and his female partner, stripped to their first suits, were each interred up to their chins, their heads beautifully dressed and powdered, appearing not unlike two very fine cauliflowers. These human plants remained in this whimsical situation six hours.

FEEL THE VITAL FLAME!

The phenomenal interest generated by James Graham's bed inspired numerous articles, essays and even satires like *The Celestial Bed* which appeared in 1781. Although published anonymously, it is believed that Graham himself wrote the following lines as part of his unquenchable desire for publicity.

> Libertines and debauchees,
> Thither haste with knocking knees;
> Genial and prolific fires,
> Shall wake your pulse to new desires;
> Tho' your embers should be dead,
> Stretch on the celestial bed;
> Soon you feel the vital flame,
> Rushing thro' your icy frame!
> Fann'd by agents all divine!
> Who condescend with him to dine.
>
> Barren Does in crowds resort,

To the Quack's imperial court;
Sweeter, lovelier you'll seem,
When you get a touch from him;
In your husband's doating eyes
You shall prove a precious prize;
His magnetic influence
Ev'ry hour new joys dispense.

THE MAP OF BEAUTY

Sir Francis Galton (1822–1911) was a Victorian pioneer of the science of eugenics, or selective breeding, and relentlessly tried to persuade people to 'breed like racehorses in order to produce a super race'. But this was not the full extent of the nobleman from Birmingham's eccentricity: he also had a passion for classifying and measuring things. Among his projects were *The Weights of British Noblemen During the Last Three Generations*, *A Method for Numerically Measuring the Degree of Resemblance between Two People* and *The Honesty of Nations*. On the last-named, Sir Francis's research led him to conclude (surprise, surprise!) that Britain came top while the town of Salonika in Greece was 'the centre of gravity of lying'. His travels also took him to Africa where – surprise again! – the nobleman found himself fascinated by the voluptuous naked figures of the women. But when he tried to use a tape measure on the village beauties, Sir Francis quickly found himself in danger of his life from their menfolk and instead devised a method of measuring their breasts, waists and hips using *a ship's sextant.*

The most curious of Galton's projects, however, was his *Beauty Map of the British Isles* published in 1850. In compiling this, he travelled from one end of the country to the other, eyeing up the female population. He later reported his findings in his Rabelaisian biography *Memories of My Life* (1908): 'Every woman I saw I classified as "beautiful", "middling" or "ugly". My conclusions as to the incidence of beauty were that London had the prettiest girls and Aberdeen the ugliest. Much to my amazement, the Map proved a great success with patrons in Aberdeen!'

A FORM OF INSANITY

The Greeks are said to have been the first to recognise the symptoms of nymphomania in women – 'an exaggerated sexual desire for male partners', according to one definition – though whether they invented anything like the device illustrated on page 150 which was allegedly built for young widows and wives whose husbands were away soldiering is doubtful. The earliest book on the subject is *Nymphomania! or, A Dissertation concerning the Furore Euterinus*, written by a certain 'J.D.T. Bienville' and published in Paris in 1840. Less than a decade later, William Acton, the intrepid investigator of prostitution in London, who believed most women had no sexual feelings, could still confess in a lecture to other medical men:

> I admit, of course, the existence of sexual excitement terminating even in nymphomania, a form of insanity which

LA ROUE
DE LA FORTUNE
Gravée fur une Cornaline.

those accustomed to visit lunatic asylums must be fully conversant with; but with these sad exceptions, there can be no doubt that sexual feeling in the female is in the majority of cases in abeyance, and even if roused (which in many instances it never can be) is very moderate compared with that of the male . . .

THE CURE FOR OOPHOROMANIA

Ladies in America who felt they might be suffering from nymphomania – or epilepsy or insanity, for that matter – had a certain Dr Robert Battey to thank for a supposed cure. At least that is what the aptly named surgeon claimed in the 1880s in a series of lectures describing his findings and his intentions. Naming the process 'Battey's Operation', he said that the process required the removal of both female ovaries in order to cure a whole range of diseases – fictional or otherwise – which he categorised as 'Oophoromania', 'Oophoralgia', 'Oophorectomy' and so on. According to L.D. Longo in his study *The Rise and Fall of Battey's Operation* (1979), thousands of women actually allowed themselves to have perfectly normal ovaries removed by the surgeon, and he adds:

> Battey was also the first man in medical history to try to induce the menopause deliberately, surgically – as a cure. His reason was thus: 'I have hoped through the intervention of the great nervous revolution which ordinarily accompanies the climacteric, to uproot and remove serious sexual disorders and re-establish general health.

Battey by name and batty by nature . . .

LIGHT ON THE SUBJECT

Couples who over-indulged in sex around the turn of this century had at least one means to turn to for revitalising their flagging libido. These were the products of firms like the Electric Life Invigorator Company who sold a range of electrically powered 'reinvigorating machines and body harnesses'. The good folk at this company – one of a number of such firms who operated on both sides of the Atlantic as the typical advertisements on these pages show – also produced a sex instruction manual coyly entitled *Nature's Revelations for the Married Only*, issued in 1904,

which, though not directly advocating sexual excess, certainly promoted the rejuvenating power of its products to anyone who might have done! The best-selling booklet – costing one shilling (5p) – exhorted its customers:

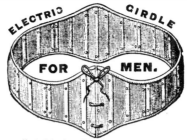

DR. SCOTT'S ELECTRIC GIRDLE FOR MEN.

Professional men affirm that there is hardly a disease which Electricity and Magnetism will not benefit or cure.

Dr. W. A. HAMMOND, of N. Y., late Surgeon-Gen. of the U. S., an eminent authority, publishes almost miraculous cures made by him with these agencies.

Most of the above Remarks apply equally to

The Electric Girdle for Gentlemen. It is a long felt want, possessing wonderful curative powers and life-giving properties. The debilitated particularly should wear them at once, and those now enjoying robust health should also wear them as a preventative of disease. They brace up and invigorate the whole system, and their vitalizing influence is quickly felt.

The pleasures of intercourse must be mutual for that which is not reciprocal must in measure be demoralising and unhealthy . . .

No healthy woman will refuse intercourse when it is right and proper . . .

Intercourse cannot be agreeable if the husband's premature emissions prevent the orgasm of the woman and the ejaculation of semen of the man in the same instant . . .

So long as a wife does not have a tired body and lacerated person which was subjected to a mistaken sense of manliness on the wedding night, and is not the victim of selfish husbandly excess, mutual pleasure is a matter that needs no instruction . .

On the last page of the booklet, a note 'begged to inform readers' that the Electric Life Invigorator Company had a number of specially trained members of its staff – 'who can be relied upon for their discretion in all personal matters' – and were ever alert to offer guidance to any troubled correspondent on 'the wonderful remedial application of electricity'.

BUST DEVELOPERS

Inventions to increase the size of female breasts are by no means a modern phenomenon. Silicone implants may be the latest fashion,

NO MORE BUSTLESS WOMEN.

HOW TO CREATE 8oz. TO 1lb. OF FIRM HEALTHY FLESH UPON BUST, NECK, ARMS, OR SHOULDERS IN FOUR WEEKS.

To introduce Latest Scientific Triumph in This Country, Complete Information and Instructions will be sent to 1,000 Readers of "The Premier Magazine."

Dr. Colonnay, the distinguished physician of the Faculty of Medicine, Paris, has at last made public the secret of his latest discovery. All readers of the French medical publications and journals devoted to feminine interests are now familiar with the astonishing results of his unique experiment upon 200 ladies, ranging from sixteen to sixty years of age, some of them in the most weakly and anæmic state of health, and all absolutely lacking in bust development. Within five days the rapid growth of new flesh was noticeable in all cases. In three to six weeks busts that were flabby, sagging, and almost non-existent had developed from 5in. to 8in. by actual measurement. Convincing statistical evidence shows that in 46 per cent. of the cases patients were compelled to stop treatment within four weeks on account of threatened over-development.

These photographs show more plainly than any words how an angular, masculine figure may now be quickly transformed to one of beautiful curves by means of the new method explained in this article.

Dr. Colonnay was the first to discover that various medicines, nostrums, prescriptions, dieting, apparatus, appliances, greasy creams, massage, and other expensive advertised methods always fail because they overlook the basic fact that the mammary glands of the bust are the only organs which lie idle the greater part of a woman's lifetime, hence they can never be developed like muscles. A full description of just how this triumph of modern science causes new, firm, and healthy tissue to be created at will, and just why its stimulating action is exerted only upon the bust, neck, shoulders, or arms, but never upon abdomen, hips, or other parts of the body, would require more space than is available for this special article, but arrangements have just been made whereby readers of THE PREMIER MAGAZINE are enabled to obtain all necessary information by promptly using coupon below. There is no charge for this, but, if convenient, two penny stamps may be enclosed for posting expenses.

IMPORTANT NOTICE.—Readers are particularly cautioned not to use this new method where more flesh is not desired, as the enlargement, when once produced, is absolutely permanent, and cannot be reduced afterwards. It is usually advisable to stop treatment about three days before the bust attains the exact size and firmness desired, as the stimulating effect may continue for two or three days, but never longer.

FREE COUPON

FRENCH BUST DEVELOPING METHOD

Coupon positively void after July 31.

Entitling (name)..

Address..
to receive under plain, sealed cover, absolutely free of cost, full particulars in regard to new method for developing the bust to any desired size and firmness.

Enclose this coupon or mention number given below, as evidence that you are entitled to accept this offer, which is exclusively for the benefit of PREMIER MAGAZINE readers. Only one member of each family may apply.

Address: MARGARETTE MERLAIN, Secretary,
Pembroke House, Oxford Street, London, W.
PREMIER MAGAZINE Coupon No. 252 C.

CREMED BUST LOTION

"I am more than thrilled since I tried and proved Milo-Creme Lotion"
—KORKY KELLY, (Noted New York Model.)

If you yearn for a shapely bust and the opportunities of having others look at you with admiration, then MILO-CREME may be just the thing for you. Contains 30,000 int units of Estrogenic Hormones that Science now reveals may be absorbed by the skin of the breasts. Easy and simple to apply.

SEND NO MONEY. Pay Postman only $2.00 plus Postal Charges on delivery, or enclose $2.00 and we will pay all charges. REMEMBER, we guarantee unconditionally that if you are dissatisfied for any reason, we will make an immediate refund. Full directions—sent in a plain box. 3 months supply $5.00.

MILO LABORATORIES DEPT. M-18
225 West 34 St.   New York 1, N. Y.

but for centuries women in any number of Western countries tried all sorts of deceptions to enhance their bosoms, mainly with padding or flattering dresses. In fact, devices to develop the bust only really became a science during the Victorian era. Among the items discreetly offered to ladies in Europe and America were a variety of creams, several types of rubber pumps, and even one or two painful stretching devices. Perhaps the most bizarre 'Bust Developer' was one registered at the US Patent Office on 5 February 1901 and given the patent number 667,447. The specifications accompanying the plans state:

This invention embraces certain improvements designed to

For BUST BEAUTY
PRO-FORMA Tablets

For beautiful bust development. To firm up, round out and increase the bosom without increase in weight or of any other measurement. Medically and scientifically tested and now prescribed by many Doctors for weak, sagging and undeveloped busts—even if caused through nursing. 100% safe (Public Analyst's report). No harmful drugs, no hormones, no exercising and nothing to wear. Just 3 Tablets a day until results achieved—usually 6 to 12 weeks. 30/- (6 WEEKS SUPPLY). Send coupon below.

enlarge the female bust. In using the device, the open end of the casing is placed against the body, around the parts to be treated, and pressed tightly there against, so as to prevent the passage of air between the body of the user and the casing. At this time the pump will be in the position shown in Figure 1 – that is to say, in its retracted position.

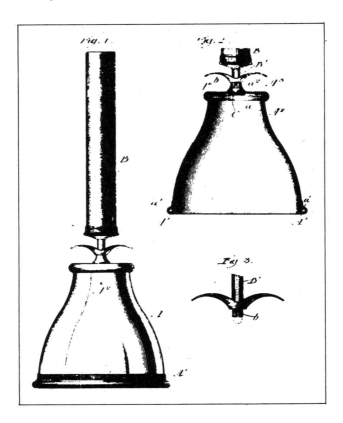

Upon extending or pulling out the pump, as Figure 2, the air is exhausted from the casing and the parts enclosed by the rim of the casing are subjected for the desired time to the influence of the vacuum, with the result that the supply of blood to the parts being treated is increased. The repetition of this treatment tends to an increased growth or an enlargement of the bust.

After the parts have been subjected to the influence of the vacuum for the desired time, the relief-aperture a^2 is uncovered, as Figure 3, thereby permitting the entrance of air to the interior of the casing, so that said casing may easily be removed.

And soon she'll be bustin' out all over . . .

THE TOOL FOR THE JOB

Massage has been a prelude to sex since ancient times. Hand massage is today, of course, considered something of an art, but in America in 1916 an inventor came up with what he believed to be the ultimate mechanical contrivance for the job. Called simply 'A Massage Apparatus', the description which accompanied the diagram lodged at the US Patent Office is a masterpiece of double meaning:

The primary purpose of my invention is to devise a tool which will mechanically stimulate the rubbing action of a hand massage for the purpose of reducing flesh. Mechanical massage heretofore has been impracticable for the reason that where a tool has been used, it was almost impossible for the user to apply the tool to all parts of the body. This is accomplished mechanically by the construction of a tool adapted to surround the body of the user and which is expansible, whereby the tool will conform to the contour of the body of the user in its reciprocating movement . . .

Phew!

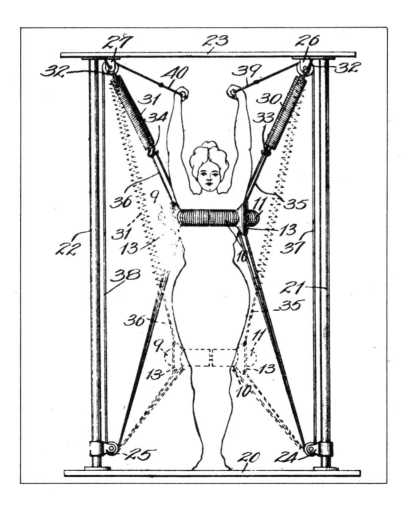

THE SEX ODYSSEY

In 1973, a South American anthropologist, Dr Santiago Geneves, set up a project to see how six young and healthy men and five beautiful women cast adrift on a raft would cope with their natural urges. The raft was well stocked with provisions and for 101 days it and the human guinea pigs were left to their own devices. Later, Dr Geneves reported: 'We asked the volunteers to monitor the mating drive while exposed to the daily hardships at sea and the enforced company of members of the opposite sex. Among the men was a Roman Catholic priest bound by a vow of chastity. Our conclusions were that sex can become a problem.'

Prize for the understatement of the year?

GOING FOR THE GROIN

A number of devices to prevent rape have also been filed with Patent Offices during recent years. The majority are designed to mutilate the penis of an assailant and though considered impractical by experts, make amusing – if uncomfortable – reading. Especially if you are a man.

'Anti-Rape Device' invented by Charles Barlow, USA, 1977. Designed to be inserted into the vagina, it contains three spears with harpoon-like barbs which will embed themselves into the penis. The rapist will be unable to remove them without medical assistance . . .

'Female Protective Device' invented by George Vogel, USA, 1980. This large piece of metal with a solid spear in the centre is to be worn under the clothes and over the vagina . . .

'Penis Locking and Lacerating Vaginal Insert' invented by Alston Levesque, USA, 1981. The vaginal insert contains sharp elements of plastic which move only inwards causing the sexual attacker to find himself inextricably trapped in the device . . .

'The Pouch Sheath' invented by Anna G. Pennystone, USA, 1983. A rigid sheath to be inserted into the vagina. The interior is coated with an adhesive and contains a pouch of chemicals which burn the penis on contact. The sheath remains affixed to the penis when it is withdrawn . . .

'The Sedative Insert' invented by Joel Rumph and Lynda Warren, USA, 1994. When positioned in the vagina, this device will inject the penis of an attacker with a fast-working sedative leaving him almost immediately incapacitated . . .

In an apt comment that neatly rounds off this section, a gynaecologist, Dr Shirley Bond, has dismissed most of these inventions as being 'obviously designed to be big enough to house an erect penis . . . in which case they would have to be so big as to make wearing them uncomfortable or even dangerous'. She added: 'You might as well opt for the medieval chastity belt – stop the penis getting in there in the first place!'

7.

FRENCH LETTERS AND ENGLISH OVERCOATS

Though the very survival of humanity is dependent on sex and procreation, the prevention of babies – contraception – has engaged the ingenuity of men and women since times immemorial. Now, of course, safe sex has become a reality (generally speaking), though not without the emergence over the years of a variety of ingenious ideas that ranged from the bizarre to the absurd and even the plain comical. The following pages are devoted to how we've kept the fun in sex and the offspring out . . .

The second-century Greek physician with the unfortunate name, Soranus, who made his home town of Ephesus something of a centre for the study of human sexuality, is regarded by a number of experts as the first great gynaecologist. He is also one of the first men to have written down methods of contraception. Though nearly two thousand years old, some of the methods he describes are still observed in certain parts of the world:

> Prevention may be achieved by anointing the *os uteri* with oil, honey, cedar gum, either alone or mixed with white lead or with alum. Soft wool introduced into the *os uteri* or the use of astringent or occlusive pessaries before coition are effective since they, too, close the *os*.
>
> Here is another method. The woman should, at the moment of ejaculation, hold her breath, draw her body back a little so as to impede entry of the semen into her uterus, then immediately sit up with bent knees and make herself sneeze. She should then clean the vagina and drink cold water.

A sneeze in time saves . . .

THE HOLE TRUTH

At the time when Soranus was making his notes, there were also known to be a number of other contraceptive ideas floating around in Greece. Oil made from wild thyme rubbed on the private parts was said to be effective, while any woman who plucked out or shaved off her pubic hair was believed to be less likely to become pregnant until she allowed it to grow again. But one idea that almost matches the sneezing ploy deserves a special mention: 'If a woman clasps a rounded pebble with a hole through the middle in her right hand while she is having coition, she will not conceive.'

THE DEER SKIN PATCH

The Romans knew all about the contraceptive sneeze – and had a fair number of other strange ideas, too. Although there was no such thing as sexual equality at that time – men dominated all areas of Roman society – the women put into practice a number of ideas in the hope of avoiding pregnancy. They were, in the main, 'pure mumbo-jumbo' according to Norman Gelb in his book *The Irresistible Impulse* (1979), in which he describes several of the most bizarre:

> A woman was advised to wear the liver of a cat in a container attached to her left foot to avoid conception, or hold her breath at the moment of sexual climax or to squat or sneeze soon afterward. If she spat three times into the mouth of a frog, she would not conceive for a year. She could avoid conception by extracting a certain substance from a spider, wrapping it in a patch of deer skin, and applying the package to her skin just before dawn.

The original morning-after method?

THE SWEET SOLUTION

The ancient Egyptians also had a variety of methods to prevent conception that were equally strange. A mixture of pomegranate crushed with rock salt and alum taken with wine before going to bed was one popular solution. Pessaries made from gum and goat's bladders were familiar in the homes of the nobles, but the sure-fire method said to have been reserved for the royal families was perhaps the most unpleasant.

Their pessaries were made from *crocodile dung*!

KEEP TAKING THE TADPOLES

The inscrutable Chinese were equally ingenious in their means of birth control. A contraceptive formula as disclosed in an ancient document from the Ming dynasty reads as follows: 'To prevent childbearing. Place a small measure of quicksilver into a bowl and to this add 16 fresh tadpoles. Fry the tadpoles until darkened and store carefully. The mixture to be taken by the woman immediately after coition has occurred.'

THE TASTE OF SUCCESS

In Europe, from the Middle Ages until well into the seventeenth century, there were a trio of weird contraceptive ideas. One of the oldest recommended that a woman should eat some bees immediately after she had had sex. Slightly less dangerous was to drink a pint of raw onion juice, or else for a lover to tuck into a whole cabbage as soon as she got up. Another idea which was apparently sold in sealed packets all over Britain during the eighteenth century by hawkers was claimed to be 'The True and Reliable Method to Prevent the Generation of Children'. It had apparently originated with the Arabs and its instructions to those women who had been foolish enough to part with their money were simplicity itself. *Jump backwards seven or nine times immediately after coition.*

Assuming they had the energy, of course . . .

TRIALS OF CHASTITY

Man is generally agreed to be the only living creature who has found reasons for deliberately inhibiting his sexual drive . . . and making a virtue out of it. Priests of the early Christian Church, in particular, promoted lives of love and chastity suggesting, in what might well be viewed as a rather self-serving manner, that the best way of achieving this was to sleep with *at least two young virgins in bed with you.* These 'trials of chastity' – as they were known –

inspired St John Chrysostom to write an essay, *Against Those Who Keep Virgins in their Houses* (c. AD 403), in which he recounted the following amusing incident:

> Our fathers only knew two forms of intimacy, marriage and fornication. Now a third form has appeared: men introduce young girls into their houses and keep them there permanently respecting their virginity. That there should really be a pleasure in this which produces a love more ardent than conjugal union may surprise you at first, but I can give proof. There was once a priest who every night slept with two virgins and challenged another priest who rebuked him for the risks he was taking to do the same. This the second man attempted to do, but although he resisted temptation he was unable to get any sleep and returned home the next day much discomforted.

A PAINFUL SOLUTION

A solution offered to the father who might find it difficult to resist such temptation – or any other male, for that matter – was offered in the pages of the curious little book entitled *Compendyous Regyment; or, A Dyetry of Health*: 'To those of my gentlemen readers possessed of an unnatural lust there are but two simple solutions. To leap into a great vessel of cold water, or to put nettles in the codpiece.'

STICKING POWER

In rural England there were for many years a number of curious beliefs about how to avoid getting pregnant. One of the most widespread of these is that a woman cannot conceive while she is breast-feeding. Young girls in Norfolk clung to an idea they would not get pregnant if they carried with them a penny stolen from a dead man – and there was a ready market for such coins of dubious authenticity until the middle years of this century.

Somerset was the source of another peculiar belief, that young men and women believed it was impossible to get pregnant if they had sex in a graveyard – especially if they were brave enough to do it 'during the midnight hour'. Perhaps the most curious of all, however, was described by Maureen Sutton in her book *We Didn't Know Aught* (1992), which focuses on sexuality and superstition in the county of Lincolnshire. She writes: 'There were women there who had no idea – or completely the wrong idea – about where babies came from. One lady, a vicar's wife, believed that contraception could be achieved by sticking plaster over her belly button.'

GOING WITH THE FLOW

A form of contraception that was evidently practised for centuries in peasant communities throughout Europe consisted of women prolonging the period of breast-feeding. Commenting on this in 1775, a German medical man aptly named Johann Peter Süssmilch – it means 'Sweet Milk' – wrote, 'Various country preachers have assured me that prolonged breast-feeding is only undertaken because of the fear of new dangers and of too many children.' Some years later, the idea was taken up again by another German, Carl Buttenstedt, who, observing that menstruation was often suspended during the breast-feeding period and pregnancy rarely happened, came up with an even stranger contraceptive method. He called it *A New Revelation in Women*, which he said promised 'complete marriage happiness'. Buttenstedt explained:

> It is necessary to stimulate the flow of milk in the breasts of non-pregnant women, even virgins, by having them sucked. This will thereby make them safe to have intercourse. Then, when children are desired, the husband or lover who performs this service – which I dare to say is hardly onerous or unpleasant for either partner – simply stops. The flow of milk will then cease and pregnancy will once again become possible . . .

A DESIRE FOR SOFT SENSATIONS

The practice of *coitus reservatus* has been acknowledged as another form of contraception in various societies for centuries. The belief that it energised and prolonged male life made it the centre of several philosophies, most notably that of an American physician, Alice Bunker Stockham, of Chicago, who named her esoteric variation 'Carezza'. She claimed in a book, *Marriage of Reform*, published in 1896, that 'Carezza' offered an 'exquisite exaltation' – even though sexual climax was never reached. As long as her instructions were followed to the letter:

> Manifestations of tenderness are indulged in without physical or mental fatigue; the caresses lead up to the connection and the sexes unite quietly and closely. Once the necessary control has been acquired, the two beings are fused and reach sublime spiritual joy. This union can be accompanied by slow controlled motions, so that voluptuous thrills do not overbalance the desire for soft sensations. If there is no wish to procreate, the storm violence of the orgasm will thus be avoided. If love is mutual, and if the 'Carezza' is sufficiently prolonged, it affords complete satisfaction, without emission or orgasm. After an hour the bodies relax, spiritual delight is increased, and new horizons are revealed with the renewal of strength . . .
>
> It is my belief that there should be an interval of two to three weeks between acts of 'Carezza', but many find that even three or four months afford a greater impetus to power and growth as well as personal satisfaction. During the interval, the thousand and one lover-like attentions give reciprocal delight and are an anticipating prophecy of the ultimate union . . .

SUPERMARKET SEX

Of course if we believe the typically idiosyncratic view of Joan Rivers, the well-known American writer and television personality, then there is really no need for contraception in bed or anywhere else for that matter – *except* in the supermarket. A few years ago she remarked: 'The only time a woman really has an orgasm is when she's shopping – otherwise she's faking it!'

FRENCH LETTERS OR ENGLISH OVERCOATS?

There has been a lot of debate over the years about just who invented the condom. In France, they believe that 'French Letters' really did originate there in the seventeenth century where they were made from fish and animal intestines. Over here, we consider that 'English Overcoats' of oil-skin deserve the accolade. The facts which stand up are these.

In 1986, five wrinkly brown condoms were found in a ruined castle at Dudley, West Midlands. Subsequently they were identified as having been brought across the Channel about 340 years ago by Royalist soldiers during the time of the Civil War. According to historians, though, they were not used by the Cavaliers for family planning, but because the men were rightly terrified of venereal disease, then known to be a killer.

In some accounts, the condom is credited as the handiwork of a French nobleman, Le Compte de Condon (1436–1513), who was also afraid of contracting syphilis at court and made himself a form of protection using goat's teats. A more likely claimant, though, is Colonel Cundum, an English officer of the Guards, who, in 1665, created an airtight oil-skin sheath which rolled back on itself into a loop to protect the regimental colours. Later, a smaller variation was used instead to protect the regiment's members – and these became known far and wide as 'English Overcoats'. So French or English? The choice is yours . . .

Casanova, the legendary womaniser, is known to have hated condoms. He preferred to insert into his partners three small gold balls which were said to prevent conception. The balls had been specially manufactured for Casanova by a goldsmith in Genoa and they served him for fifteen years without mishap – or offspring. To the sceptical, the reason was much simpler: the great lover was infertile.

Perhaps the most unusual condom of all was a French example dating from 1810 which was auctioned at Christie's in London in 1992. It was described as 'the world's most collectable condom' in a report in *The Times* of 11 June, which stated: 'The device is made of sheep's intestine and tied with a silk ribbon. It also bears what is called "a satirical ecclesiastical illustration". A member of Christie's staff explained: "It depicts a nun, two monks and a bishop. She appears to be choosing between them."'

So now, after all those years, we know what put the grin on the face of 'The Laughing Cavalier'!

BLUNTING THE SENSATIONS

The original condom was not intended as a contraceptive device at all, but as a measure against infection. This was certainly the purpose behind the linen sheath worn under the prepuce which the Italian anatomist Gabriel Fallopius (1523–62) proposed in his treatise *De Morbo Gallico*, published in 1560. He had made a special study of the organs of generation and the tube connecting the ovaries with the uterus is named after him. These sheaths were still serving the same purpose a hundred and more years later, as a physician named Daniel Turner amusingly comments in a pamphlet written in 1717: 'The *condum* is the best, if not the only Preservative, our Libertines have found out at present. And yet by reason of its blunting the Sensation, I have heard some of them acknowledge that they often chose to risk a Clap, rather than engage *cum Hastis sic clypeatis* . . .'

The ORANGERIE; or the Dutch Cupid reposing, after the fatigues of Planting. — Vide The Visions in Hampton Bower.

ARMOUR AGAINST ENJOYMENT

Some of the early contraceptive sheaths were extraordinary inventions made from a variety of materials including animal offal, sausage skins, leather and even tortoiseshell (in Japan). Some were undoubtedly worse than useless – although in 1797, the philosopher and economist Jeremy Bentham had suggested the wider use of the sheath as 'a means of reducing the poor rate' – and it was not until 1844, when the American inventor Charles Goodyear (1800–60) developed vulcanised rubber, that the modern condom became popular.

It was not only Casanova who thought the sheath was a poor sort of invention – many women shared his feelings. The French beauty Madame de Sévigné (1626–96) was particularly scornful of one type made of gold-beater's skin: 'It is an armour against enjoyment and a spider-web against danger!'

A SCANDALOUS BOOK

John Marten was an eighteenth-century quack surgeon and the

author of *Gonosologium Novum; or, A New System of all the Secret Infirmities and Diseases, Natural, Accidental, and Venereal in Men and Women* which, after its publication in 1709, caused him to be indicted before the Queen's Bench. The medical work was said to be 'evil disposed and wicked' and intended to corrupt the public. Though the charge was later dropped, Marten's work became an immediate best-seller and quickly ran into six editions. What made the book particularly intriguing was the author's claim to have invented an infallible condom. 'It is made of linen and impregnated with certain lotions of my special making. However, I shall not reveal their formula in these pages lest it give encouragement to the lewd . . .'

THE DEFLOWERING OF VIRGINS

The eighteenth-century Scottish physician and writer William Buchan (1729–1805) is credited with being the first to denounce what was regarded as a widespread 'truth' that a man could be cured of venereal disease by deflowering a virgin! This bizarre belief had apparently been cruelly put into practice for many years in parts of Great Britain and a number of European countries before Buchan exposed it as nonsense in his pamphlet *Observations Concerning the Prevention and Cure of the Venereal Disease* (1796):

> One of the most absurd notions that ever entered the mind of man is that a disease may be cured by communicating it to another – in this case by having sexual intercourse with a virgin. Yet in many countries this is believed, and is at present in this, with regard to the venereal disorder. We might as well suppose that one mad-dog, by biting another, would receive a cure; or, that the wretch expiring under the plague, would recover by communicating the disease to those around him. It would be difficult to say whether an attempt to obtain a cure by communicating the disease to another is more wicked or absurd.

KEEPING CLEAN AND KIND

Among a spate of sex instruction manuals published at the dawn of the nineteenth century – including *The Delights of Love* (1804) and *The Art of Making Love in More Ways Than One* (1813) – was the innocuous-sounding *Every Woman's Book* (1826) which actually dealt very frankly with problems of contraception and offered advice on love-making: especially for 'women who are easily aroused or not at all'. It mentioned the use of sheaths, *coitus interruptus*, and a vaginal sponge – citing the example of one female aristocrat who was said never to go out to dinner without being prepared with a sponge. The book also quoted the risqué lines of John Wilmot, the libertine Earl of Rochester (1647–80), pleading with one of his bed companions:

> Fair nasty nymph, be clean and kind,
> And all my joys restore
> By using paper still behind
> And sponges for before.

A peep into . . .

. . . Madam's boudoir

THE FRENCH METHOD

Ideas of contraception were by and large given very short shrift in most Victorian manuals on 'Married Love'. Even in a letter on the topic written to a medical journal in 1853, William Acton, the London doctor who had made an exhaustive study of the city's underground world of sex and prostitution, stuck firmly to the traditions of the age by withholding from his fellow practitioners any details of the method in question:

> I must direct the attention of the profession to the dangers that married couples could incur in defrauding nature by practices that have been called 'Conjugal Onanism'. A Mr. Bergeret has in a French work entitled, *Les Fraudes de l'Accomplissement des Fonctions Generatrices* given a very succinct account of how it is that French parents determine (and carry out) that they shall have only one, or at most two, children. So serious, indeed, is the paroxysm of the nervous system produced by the sexual

spasm that its immediate effect is not always unattended with danger, and I know of men with weak hearts who have died in the act.

It is a far, far better thing that I do . . .

A STANDING OVATION

One of the leading figures in the fight to ban promiscuity in America during the later years of the nineteenth century was the New York clergyman Reverend Harvey Newcomb, who wrote books, pamphlets and delivered hundreds of lectures all aimed at the nation's young men. His most frequently voiced piece of advice to avoid temptation was this: 'When you feel any inclination to go abroad in search of forbidden pleasures with members of the other sex, sit down with your sisters at the piano and sing "Home, Sweet Home".'

MY LIFE AND MANY LOVES

One man who made a lifetime career out of promiscuity was the Irish-born writer Frank Harris (1856–1931), who has been described by one of his biographers as 'an incorrigible liar, vociferous boaster, an unscrupulous philanderer with the aspect and outlook of a typical melodrama "Sir Jasper" and an obsession with sex'. In his own volumes of autobiography, *My Life and Loves* (1923–27) – which were banned for years as pornographic – Harris presented himself as one of the world's foremost lovers and authorities on sex. But historian Hugh Kingsmill told a rather different story in 1932:

> The book contains an astonishing amount of sexual misinformation. Among other things, Harris believed that a woman's 'safe' period was exactly midway between menstruations, that there was no danger from impregnation

from second and third repetitions of the sex act, that a water douche would kill sperm, and that nocturnal emissions were debilitating. As a young man, he apparently once 'cured' himself of such emissions by a piece of string, tied tightly.

IF THE CAP FITS . . .

The work of the famous British pioneer of birth control, Marie Stopes (1880–1958), and the storm of controversy which surrounded the publication of her book *Married Love* in 1918, is well known. Initially a lecturer on fossil plants and coal mining, she became alarmed at the ignorance of men and women about sex in married life and in 1921 founded her Society and Pioneer Clinic for Constructive Birth Control, which recommended the cervical cap for family planning – later to be largely replaced by the Pill. Not all of Dr Stopes' views – a few were quite eccentric – were accepted by the rest of the medical profession and two are worth mentioning here. One, it seems, answers a mystery encountered earlier in the book . . .

When the fluid from the male prostate is absorbed by the woman, it has a tonic, health-giving effect . . .

In bed, it is comparatively unimportant whether the head or feet are at the north end of the bed, but it is very important that the body should lie south-north or north-south . . .

A PEA-BRAINED SCHEME

In 1928, a German doctor, Heinrich Detlen, claimed in a series of advertisements to have developed a perfect 'morning after' contraceptive. He called it 'Anti-Baby Marmalade' and instructed customers to take two spoonfuls on their breakfast slice of bread. For months, his business in Munich flourished, until complaints reached the ears of the police from enraged women – all of whom had become pregnant – that the marmalade didn't work. A contemporary report reveals the finale: 'Dr. Detlen was arrested and certain tests carried out on his product. The paste was found to consist mainly of peas . . .'

INCOMPLETE ELIMINATION . . .

The famous British thriller writer Eric Ambler (1909–98) initially worked in an advertising agency writing slogans for various products – including the breakfast cereal for which he coined the immortal line 'Snap, Crackle and Pop' – until the success of his first book, *The Mask of Dimitrios* (1939), rewrote the spy genre and freed him to become a full-time writer. A *Times* journalist, James Fenton, has recalled one particular campaign that Ambler worked on and the extraordinary sexual fallacy it created:

> He had been given the *Exlax* account at a time when the slogan for this laxative chocolate was: '*Exlax* – For Incomplete Elimination'. The theory was that an inefficient excretory system caused a poisoning of the body. *Exlax* made sure you got rid of everything. But Mr. Ambler's researchers revealed that people were buying the stuff under a misapprehension. They thought 'Incomplete Elimination' was a sexual dysfunction which could be cured with chocolate!

. . . COMPLETE ELIMINATION

It may seem extraordinary today, but half a century ago the sale of contraceptives from slot machines was considered 'an open invitation to juveniles to indulge in indiscriminate sexual intercourse' according to a number of members of the British Parliament who urged the Home Secretary, Mr Chuter Ede, to put a stop to all such merchandising. On 21 October 1949, *The Times* reported the outcome: 'Mr. Ede, Home Secretary, announced in the House of Commons today, amid general cheers, that a model by-law prohibiting the sale of contraceptives from automatic machines, would be circulated to all county and county borough authorities for adoption by them.'

THE COMING OF THE PILL

The announcement that a completely new form of contraceptive – the Pill, to be taken orally – was undergoing clinical trials in 1960, prompted many differing and heated opinions. Although one reader of the medical journal *The Lancet*, Oliver Jelly, accepted that a safe method of birth control *was* desirable, there were other dangers that he felt must not be ignored.

The method offends by not being an open and unconcealed contract between the parties. It is possible that either the man

BUY DIRECT
Enormous Saving on
SANITARY RUBBER GOODS
for men. Finest Grade Latex products at
less than ⅓ retail prices. Sample dozen 35c,
4 dozen assorted $1.00, gross $2.50. Fresh
guaranteed stock. Illustrated catalog of 1000
Bargains 10c. Catalog and valuable gift
items FREE with $1 order. Sent in plain
wrapper. Order today.
RELIABLE PRODUCTS, Dept. 331
504 S. Crawford Ave.   Chicago, Ill.

Use Time Proven G.M. & S. Products
Scientifically prepared and patented. For
Irregularity when Nature Fails. Speedy and
effective in relieving some of the most dis-
couraging cases. GUARANTEED, PURE
AND HARMLESS Vegetable and Herb In-
gredients. Favored by Doctors and Thousands
of Thankful Women. No interference. POST-
PAID, Plain Sealed Wrapper Marked "PER-
SONAL." Formula No. 1—$2.00. A SPE-
CIAL FORMULA No. 2, compounded for
Chronic, Stubborn cases, $5.00. Write
Madame D for trial size and complete Hygiene
Catalogue, 25c.
QUALITY PRODUCTS
3301 Beach Ave.   Dept. B-5   Chicago, Ill.

Sanitary Goods. SAFELY THIN. Guar. 5
years against Deterioration. 24 asstd., $1.00;
5 doz., $2.00; a gross, $14.00. SPECIAL—
Three Doz. Sample Asstd. $1.00. Sent in
PLAIN WRAPPER marked "PERSONAL."
Handy Metal Case "FREE" with all orders.
Illust. Catalog & Samples, 10c. Large Trial
Pkg., 25c.
QUALITY PRODUCTS
3301 Beach Ave.   Chicago, Ill.

GENUINE   LIQUID   LATEX
. . . STERILIZED . . .
SUPERSENSITIVE
Special 4 Doz. Assortment $1. Prepaid
in plain wrapper marked "Personal."
FREE! Beautiful Metal Pocket Container
with 3 rolled Prophylactics with every $1
order.
Men's and Women's personal specialties, Sex
Books, etc. Send 10c for Sample and Illus-
trated catalog.
BOSWELL PRODUCTS, Dept. L-1
159 N. State Street   Chicago, Ill.

UP TO 800% PROFIT SELLING
RUBBER GOODS
Guaranteed SUPERSENSITIVE
Send for agents' outfit consisting of 30 as-
sorted samples from the LEADING FAC-
TORIES, with retail value of from $5.00 to
$7.00, shipped by express PAID in a plain
package, sent on the receipt of $1.00 to cover
cost of packing and shipping charges. This
refunded on your first $10.00 order.
ARTEE CO.
Dept. R.G.   Upper Darby, Pa.

RUBBER GOODS
Best quality. Texide Brand. Thin, strong,
supersensitive. $1.00 dozen. Sent prepaid in
plain cover.
SHERELL PRODUCTS
92 Norwood   Rochester, N. Y.

181

or woman could see that the pill is taken, or given surreptitiously without concern or knowledge of the other; or, worse, it could be given by an outside agent either for public or private purposes . . .

The other complications such as genital or mammary cancer, risk of mutation, etc, will presumably be found out later. But it seems to me that a profession which is prepared to handle this drug in this country is betraying a sacred heritage. The opportunity is still open – refuse now to handle it, before it is too late!

In time, of course, the Pill became an accepted – and acceptable – part of modern sex life, but not before it was the subject of a fierce debate in the House of Commons in June 1966. During this, the Minister of Health, Mr Kenneth Robinson, was asked a question by Mrs Renee Short, Labour MP for Wolverhampton North East, which suggested there was a comic aspect to the public acceptance of the oral contraceptive: 'Some general practitioners are requiring written consent of the husband before prescribing oral contraceptives to women patients. Will you issue a directive to stop this feudal practice?'

In reply, the Minister said he was 'not sure whether this was a matter for him'.

IT'S THE REAL THING . . .

Over the past century there have been many kinds of douche put forward as an ideal means for preventing conception, from the coyly named 'Hygienic Whirling Spray Syringe' which was introduced to the Victorians and remained popular until the thirties, to the multi-flavoured, lip-smacking douches like Raspberry, Cherry, Tutti-Frutti and, especially, Cola, which became an international fad in the sixties and is still going down strong in certain parts of the world today.

The Cola douche was much discussed in magazines aimed at American teenagers in the sixties and inspired letters like this one,

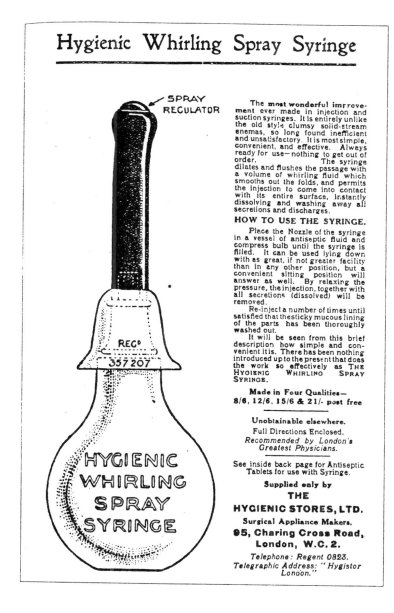

written by 'A. Nony Mouse' (sic) from Seattle, to the medical columnist of *Teen Dreams* in June 1961:

> Dear Doctor – I have been told that if a girl douches with cola after sex, the acid in it will kill the sperms. This seems to be true

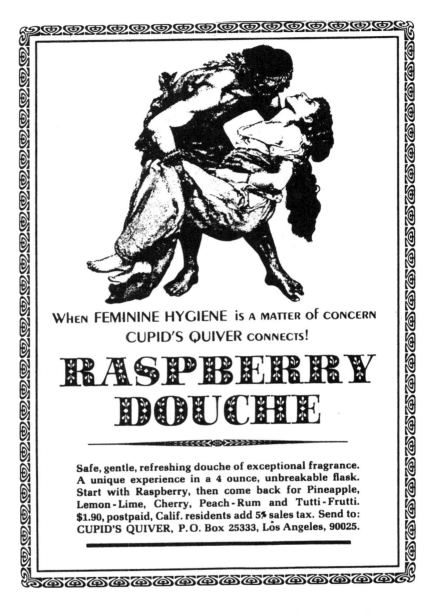

When FEMININE HYGIENE is a matter of concern
CUPID'S QUIVER connects!

RASPBERRY DOUCHE

Safe, gentle, refreshing douche of exceptional fragrance.
A unique experience in a 4 ounce, unbreakable flask.
Start with Raspberry, then come back for Pineapple,
Lemon - Lime, Cherry, Peach - Rum and Tutti - Frutti.
$1.90, postpaid, Calif. residents add 5% sales tax. Send to:
CUPID'S QUIVER, P.O. Box 25333, Los Angeles, 90025.

for me and my boyfriend as we have been having sex for a year
and I have not missed a period. Is this just a coincidence or is
it really effective?

Answer: The carbon dioxide in cola dissolves in water and

forms carbonic acid which is slightly acid in reaction. This definitely does inhibit the movement of sperm. However, the carbonated soda might force itself into your womb, setting up an infection. Furthermore, neither this nor any other form of douche is a really reliable form of birth control.

According to recent reports, the use of cola as a douche is now 'one of the most common and successful forms of contraceptive in Third World countries . . .'

SAVING ON MEN

In 1965, Paul Pawlowski, a Polish-born engineer living in England, published a leaflet proposing a bizarre way to cut down the birth-rate without any form of contraception at all: seven men sharing one woman. The document, which he mailed to leading doctors and a number of British medical associations, put forward the case for 'Pawlowski's Polyandry':

It is my intention to find another six men and one woman to start Polyandry . . .

Polyandry produces fewer babies because it means that seven men marry one woman who can only have one baby per year . . .

Taking the average weekly income of a man at £15, there would be £105 a week to support our wife and offspring . . .

THE KEY TO PLEASURE . . .

In a hark-back to the long-running British TV quiz show *Take Your Pick*, in which contestants had the choice of opening a mystery box which might contain anything from a fortune to a dried prune, a French condom manufacturer began offering in

1989 boxes of condoms which came with two keys. The instructions which accompanied the boxes read: 'One key is for each partner in the relationship. This will ensure mutual consent at all times.'

A case of 'When Opportunity Knocks . . .'

ONE ENORMOUS BANG AFTER ANOTHER . . .

To many people, the British Houses of Parliament are also a long-running comedy show. Certainly, over the years, sex has reared its ugly head in the course of a number of debates in both chambers. Perhaps, though, the most unintentionally funny comment was made in the House of Commons in 1979 during a debate on working conditions and the need for leave of absence for both men and women on specific occasions. It was made by the Conservative MP, Ian Gow: 'If paternity leave were granted, it would result in a direct incitement to a population explosion.'

THE SEAT OF THE PROBLEM

The lavatory has been the villain of the piece in a number of odd sexual fallacies. For years in Britain, naive young girls believed it was possible to get pregnant if they sat on the lavatory immediately after a man had used it; and, in America, there was a fad during the fifties that to pee in a male toilet after having sex would somehow act as a contraceptive! In his book *The World's Worst Medical Mistakes* (1996), Martin Fido says the tradition has now been updated for the nineties: 'Lavatory seat covers and telephone covers have both been marketed as a guard against AIDS, though the condition cannot be acquired from either source. Weirder still was the offer of an AIDS-preventative toaster visor!'

VARIETY IS THE SPICE OF SEX LIFE

Contraceptives have come in many unusual shapes and sizes over the years. In the late nineteenth century, for example, a range of British condoms bore the likeness of Queen Victoria – who was the mother of *nine* children, of course – while a popular American brand, *Ramses*, was named after the great pharaoh Ramses II, who is said to have fathered no fewer than 160 offspring! More recently in 1994, an Italian, Lini Missio, patented a 'super-safe' condom that was coated with a substance that changed electrical conductivity if it was torn or damaged and set off a microchip that produced a warning sound. The most popular version played Beethoven! Still more recently, *The Times* of 16 April 1999 carried this item under the heading 'Bedtime Cocoa': 'The Vegan Society has approved a range of condoms made without animal ingredients or derivatives. Milk protein is used in the production of latex for most condoms, but the German firm Condomi uses cocoa powder instead in the new range.'

And with that – sleep well! Unless you have something else on your mind after all this stimulation . . .

8.

Sex In Space

One question remains to be asked at the dawn of a new millennium. With all the progress in science and medicine, are sexual fallacies and fads a thing of the past? If the evidence of the previous pages, which cover some two thousand and more years of human history, are anything to go by, the answer would seem to be a resounding 'No!' As long as sex is a pleasure – and why on earth shouldn't it be? – there will always be men and women on the planet looking for new diversions and devices. And more than likely into the beyond, now that we are fast conquering space.

Writers have, of course, been speculating on the future for years. Where the immediate century is concerned, Aldous Huxley suggested over fifty years ago in *Brave New World* (1932) a society of human robots who satisfy their senses with films called 'feelies'. More recently, the French artist Jean-Claude Forest pictured in his controversial comic strip *Barbarella* (1962; filmed in 1968) a future world where a 'Pleasure Machine' will be able to satisfy any sexual fantasy, no matter how exotic or erotic.

Indeed, science fiction writers have been busy speculating about future sex for a while. The leading American proponent, James Blish (1921–75), in particular, has written at length about 'the technological possibilities, as yet untapped, of lifting man out of the stone age of sensual pleasure'. He claims that the 'direct, private pleasures of the sense have not undergone any really significant changes throughout the ages' – and this must surely soon come (if you'll pardon the expression). A selection of the more amusing and bizarre of the prophecies for future sex are to be found in this final section of the book . . .

CYBERSEX

In 1969, a group of scientists at the Bio-Cybernetic Institute of Tokaida University in Tokyo released details of their project 'Cybersex', which smacked more than a little of the 'Pleasure Machine' in *Barbarella*. It was, in fact, a further development of an earlier project entitled 'Intersex', which had already aroused interest in several other scientific establishments working on advanced computers. Donald Kenzotaki, the leader of the project, explained their mission to provide a new form of *life-long* sexual pleasure:

> We plan to program our FOCAM 230-20 computer with a complete set of sensory and manipulative responses from a single subject, recorded during a number of varied sexual encounters. In this way, the partner need not be connected to his mate via the 'Intersex' hook-up, but need merely enter a 'Cybersex' studio, put his partner's program tape on the computer, attach the sensors and manipulators, and proceed as if in direct contact with her from a remote studio. Any action, feeling or response he might make will be instantly interpreted by the computer, which will then examine the woman's memory for the appropriate images, vocalizations, sensory responses and movements pre-recorded by the absent partner, and transmit them directly to the subject in the studio.
>
> Thus through 'Intersex' for direct sensory contact with a distant partner, and 'Cybersex' for relating personally to the tapes of distant partners, communications science may banish loneliness, separation and even death . . . and may even bring meaningful variety to the sexual life of a couple as they will be able to repeat experiences from their earliest meetings right through maturity and older age . . .

•

VIRGIN BIRTHS – FULLY COVERED

The question of virgin births has been debated for years. The early Christian Church believed that the Virgin Mary had been impregnated through her ear – and the resulting paranoia about aural sex became so widespread that the naked ear was looked upon as an erogenous zone and a fashion for tight-fitting wimples was born which lasted for hundreds of years. In 1975, a *Sunday Pictorial* request for information about virgin births produced nineteen claimants who believed their child had no father. One, apparently, could not be disproved. The most recent development in this story has been the launching of an insurance policy covering 'A Virgin Birth by Act of God'. A report from the *Financial Mail on Sunday*, 16 May 1999, explains:

> At least 15,000 women world-wide have insured against having a virgin birth at the millennium. And those called Mary or Maria are five times more likely on average to take out such cover.
>
> But women who believe they may become the mother of the second Messiah are unlikely to find a suitable policy on the standard insurance market. Goodfellow Rebecca Ingrams Pearson (GRIP) claims to be the only provider specialising in this and other unusual cover.
>
> GRIP has found that the approaching millennium has heightened concerns over unexplained phenomena and this has boosted demand for its policies. Its Alien All Risks insurance, which has sold 8,000 policies in the UK and 40,000 worldwide, provides for an annual premium of £104, £1 million of cover against being abducted or eaten by aliens, or being impregnated with their microchips.
>
> Says Simon Burgess, managing partner of GRIP, 'Many clients take the existence of aliens seriously and feel there is a high risk of abduction. We have not paid a single claim yet for alien abduction or virgin birth, but we certainly would do so for a genuine claim . . .

Shortly after the policy was launched, a spokesman of the Church Synod complained with a wry sense of humour: 'What happens if a bolt of lightning hits a condom factory and makes millions of unseen faults in condoms?'

MEN WHO GET PREGNANT

Male pregnancy is another subject that has been around for years. In some primitive societies, men would simulate birth pangs as their wives were giving birth, while the Hua tribe in the highlands of Papua New Guinea claim that some members of their tribe – both males and females – have actually seen foetuses that came from men's bodies. American anthropologist Anna Meigs, who has made a close study of this phenomenon, reported in 1994:

> Men are believed to become pregnant in three ways. They may eat a food that has been touched by a woman who is menstruating – or by a woman who has married into the community but does not yet have children. They may eat possum, the most taboo food of all – for according to the Hua, the animal jumps out of trees like a baby from its mother and has fur like pubic hair. The third factor is sorcery – a process called *Kembige* which can either cause a steady physical decline or make a man pregnant . . .

The truth about the men and their distended bellies is, according to Anna Meigs, quite simple. It's called *kwashiorkor* – and you can look it up in the dictionary if you don't know!

LORI FOPAL AND MALE MOTHERS

In April 1986, *Cosmopolitan* magazine reported that three men in Minnesota were expecting test-tube babies later in the month. The story caused something of a furore – one television programme researcher rang the magazine asking for further details. 'Some

bizarre things happen in the States,' he explained. 'They've made male baboons pregnant so why not men?' What he and many others should have spotted was that the by-line of the author, Lori Fopal, was, in fact, an anagram for April Fool!

Despite this practical joke, several prospective 'male mothers' *did* approach fertility experts after a statement by medical guru Lord Winston in March 1999 that 'modern technology could make it possible for a man to bear a child'. He sparked a nationwide debate after declaring on television that a combination of IVF techniques and surgery could implant a foetus in the abdomen of a man and, in theory, enable him to carry a pregnancy to term. Despite noting all the inevitable problems – including the possibility of massive internal bleeding, the need for female hormone treatment and fear of abnormal foetus development – the *Sunday Times* suggested that transsexuals would probably be among the first to volunteer:

> Sarah Wilson, who was born a man, said she would be willing to try such a procedure. Wilson, 32, of Greenwich, southeast London, said: 'I always think of the film *Junior* in which Arnold Schwarzenegger gets pregnant and I always wish it could be me. If I could afford it, I would go for it.'

MAKING A BOOB OF IT . . .

A letter published in the *Sunday Times* in July 1983 by a certain 'Joan Ellis of Blue Stocking All Girls, Newnham College, Cambridge' advocated the wearing of nipple rings and claimed 'breast cancer appears to be unknown in women who wear nipple rings or studs'. The writer added that the practice had existed since Victorian times and the piercing provided 'a permanent increase in sensitivity which is why young women are increasingly attracted by the idea'. A week later, the *Sunday Mirror* showed the story to have been a bit of a boob by its rival as no such person existed at the college. Nipples also got themselves into the news in another sensitive area in connection with cigarette smoking, as Dick and Rose Girling reported in *Would You Believe It, Doctor?* (1976):

> Fashionable psychology has firmly cast the cigarette in the role of nipple substitute. Support for this theory has been provided by research showing a direct link between the ability to stop smoking and the age of weaning. Those who could not kick the habit were weaned at an average age of 4.7 months; those who gave up easily, however, had not been deprived of the real thing until they were 8 months old . . .

POUNDING THE PAVEMENT IS WRONG

The problem of impotence continues to raise its head – or fails to, as the case may be – and yet another cause has been suggested: too much jogging. A group of doctors at Los Condores University in California reported in 1983 that men who pounded the pavement too much in an effort to stay healthy ran the risk of ruining their sex lives. They found that men who ran more than fifteen miles a week suffered a drop in the level of the male hormone testosterone, which governs the sex drive. And the further they ran, the more dramatic the reduction in hormone levels. Alex Horowicz, the head of sports medicine at the university, commented, 'There is no doubt that after prolonged running a man is not at the height of his sexual powers.' However, the claims were met with wry amusement by the Health Education Council in Britain. A spokesman told the press: 'We look at reports like these with interest and sometimes incredulity. I don't think people should take it too seriously – though anyone running more than 25 miles a week won't have too much energy left for sex anyway . . .'

SEXUAL DYNAMITE

According to recent reports, a chemical has been found that can combat impotence in men. The impact of this chemical is literally dynamite: because it's nitroglycerine, used in the manufacture of explosives and rocket fuel. When applied as a cream or as a drug-soaked patch, the chemical produces a significant improvement in male sexual problems. According to a report in the *Sunday Times* of 22 September 1996, 'Scientists believe that the nitroglycerine is absorbed by the body and is broken down into nitric oxide, a gas that controls erections.' But although the chemical is quite safe – it only explodes when temperatures reach 218°C – there is a downside, as Dr Fernando Borges of the St Petersburg General Hospital in Florida, who uses it in the treatment of impotence, has explained: 'Pilot trials have shown that impotent men who wear a nitroglycerine patch for two hours prior to intercourse can sustain love-making for up to three hours. However, it can cause headaches. And it can be absorbed by a partner, too, who will also complain of a headache . . .'

So *whose* excuse will the headache be now?

DIG THIS FOR SEX!

After all the centuries of providing the plants and vegetables to give sex a fillip in the shape (and ingredients) of aphrodisiacs, gardening itself has now earned a special place in the sexual lore of the millennium. According to *New Eden* magazine in its April 1999 issue, dedicated to what will be 'in' for the new century: 'Gardening is the new sex . . . One in four women prefer it to intercourse. It may not be the new rock'n'roll, but there is no denying it is hip . . .'

Gives digging the potatoes a whole new meaning!

NO RUMPY OR PUMPY

And if gardening doesn't grab you, then celibacy is 'a good millennium career move', the *Sun* newspaper told its readers that same month, insisting that abstinence was *the* new sex. Citing a number of showbusiness women who had done just that because their careers did not allow them enough time for men, the paper quoted breakfast television presenter Esther McVey: 'Rumpy-pumpy at 3.45 am is not happening for me. Anybody else would probably give it a go at 3.44 am, but I've got my heart set on a life free of both rumpy and pumpy. I thought about it long and hard.'

A return to Victorian values or just another fad?

SAFE SEX COMPETITION

Oral sex has finally become an openly discussed topic after being taboo in most countries for centuries. There are still places, however, where it is illegal: including Singapore where it is declared 'against the order of nature' *unless* it is practised as a prelude to full sex. In nearby Australia, however, things couldn't be more different – as a news item in the appropriately named magazine *Down Under* reported in January 1998:

> Australia's National Safe Sex Day is a day when all Ozzies are warmly encouraged to talk about and perform safe oral sex acts. Competitions include the 'Mintie Bum' in which competitors insert mints into their anus and walk about before a panel of judges, and the 'Safe Oral Sex Competition', performed on judges, who are charged with the onerous task of electing the King and Queen of Oral Sex . . .

LOOK WHAT'S SHOWING . . .

A curious little television documentary film, *Private Dicks: Men Exposed*, shown in America in March 1999, almost turned the clock back in one segment to those ancient stories of women being men turned inside out. It featured a transsexual who explained that in a modern sex change the penis was not chopped off, but simply turned inside out to form the walls of the vagina. The film, shot by Meema Spadola and Thom Powers – the creators of a low-budget, big hit about women's chests, *Breasts*, made in 1996 – took a trousers-down view of the male member and featured a certain Jonah Falcon who claimed to possess the longest organ in America. The most amusing comment, however, was made by another participant who said: 'The big surprise to me was that the friends of my girlfriend had more problems with me doing it than I did. I was, like, shocked that they're so possessive of their boyfriends' penises. It's like it's theirs!'

THE VENUS BABY

Stories of UFOs, alien abduction and women who claim to have been sexually abused and impregnated by visitors from other planets have become almost commonplace in recent years. The following amusing story is taken from the pages of the *Kensington Post* of 14 March 1978:

> A woman who claims she is going to have a 'baby from Venus' has puzzled Mr. George King, the leader of the Aetherius Society, a London-based society which investigates alleged contacts with aliens.
>
> 'I think she's been fiddling about with psychic matters,' says Mr. King.

Whatever happened to those little green men?

LOW-GRAVITY LOVERS

Scientists are predicting that some time soon in the present century, people will return to the Moon and begin colonisation. Aside from the marvellous opportunities this will provide for astronomy, space flight and exploration, it is expected that the little world will quickly become a mecca for tourists. On the Moon, these visitors will be able to enjoy almost unlimited recreation – although the supreme experience, it is believed, will be *sex*. For the weaker gravity there will give lovers the chance of enjoying varieties of love-making positions quite impossible on Earth, as medical scientist Dr Andrew Stanway explained to journalists in December 1994:

> The very act of making love on the Moon will last much longer than it does here, because people's bodies will move so much more slowly. And every lover will automatically be six times lighter.

Mind you, there will still be dangers for the unwary. Although weight changes on the Moon, mass does not. And exuberant lovers, artistically gliding down on their partners from a great height, will have painful falls if they miss the bed . . .

ASTRAL LUSTS

NASA, the American space agency, is, in fact, being pressed to launch a project to consider what male and female astronauts will do when the urge takes them to have sex in space. One journalist has even suggested a title, 'The Zero-G-Coupling Ecstasy Project'. With several hundred men and women having already flown on shuttle missions, the fact is that nobody has *yet* made love in space. White rats have mated – but not humans. Now, with the probability of space stations soon being in orbit for six months and two-year missions setting off for Mars, NASA is being urged to put extraterrestrial coupling on its agenda. Dr Patricia Santy, a psychiatrist at the University of Texas and a former NASA flight surgeon, has warned that it is foolish to ignore the possibility of what could happen on a long-duration space mission:

> Sex is a normal part of human behaviour. It happens in offices. It happens in the Antarctic. It happens wherever you have males and females. You put them together in something close to a singles bar atmosphere, a charged mixture of sexually unattached competitors, and it could be a disaster.
>
> Apart from the belief that weightless sex would be fun, celestial sex remains pretty much a mystery. Little is known about the chemical and biological implications. Or about such things as the effect of zero gravity on contraception. Even about the possibility or advisability of human reproduction in space. Before we go to these places, we ought to be doing preliminary experiments . . .

PS. Any potential libidonauts should write to NASA and *not* the publisher.

THE FINAL FRONTIER

A suggestion that the answer to lust in space would be single-sex missions has met with a firm thumbs down by both the American and Russian space scientists. They are agreed there should be provision rather than prohibition for the crossing of the final frontier – love among the stars. A US psychologist, Yvonne Clearwater, who, as head of a hability research group, has been working on the design of living quarters on space missions, explained recently about the need to provide for close encounters of an intimate kind:

> If we lock people up for 90-day periods we must plan for the possibility of intimate behaviour. Our job is not to serve as judges of morality, but to support people in living as comfortably and as normally as possible while doing extremely important work. There are plans for cubicles for two and agreement has been reached to soundproof them to allow privacy for sex.
>
> The easy way around it would be to run one sex stations, but there is clear evidence that mixed gender groups work more harmoniously. The whole work atmosphere and mood is better. Somehow, the women elevate the relationship in a small team and this helps to stimulate its capacity for work . . .

And once erotic frolicking begins on the high frontier, won't the next phase be space marriages, space babes and, inevitably, space divorces?

THE LAST WORD

So which of the prophecies and ideas in this section will become just fallacies or fads in the years ahead, as so many of the others in the pages of this book did in the past? Only time, the ingenuity of men and women, and the not-so-little matter of the sexual urge, will tell. The last word, though, deserves to go to the writer Ira Reiss, in his excellent book *The Encyclopedia of Sexual Behaviour* (1990): 'We are in a state of transition and those who cling to the past get hurt by the customs of the present, and those who rush to the future are damaged by the traditions of the past.'

In a phrase, always be ready to adjust your mind, your morals and not least of all your dress!

THE END!